m

THIS BOOK WAS READ BY

_____

NAME OF PARENTS, GRANDPARENTS, RELATIVES, FRIEND

TO PREPARE FOR THE BAR/BAT MITZVAH CEREMONY OF

_____

CHILD'S NAME

_____

DATE

_____

TORAH PORTION

_____

NAME OF SYNAGOGUE AND COMMUNITY

THIS BOOK WAS A GIFT FROM

_____

Bar/Bat Mitzvah Basics is for you if you are:

- A family that wants to understand what is involved from start to finish in preparing your child for a meaningful bar or bat mitzvah celebration, from the educational aspects all the way to the party planning; from the initial interview with a tutor to clearing the tables after the party. This book speaks to all parents, and it will be particularly valuable if you are:

  Not yet affiliated with a congregation (or *havurah*) but still wishing to prepare your child for a bar/bat mitzvah ceremony. It will even help you to find a congregation that meets your needs.

  The parents of a child with special learning needs.

  A member of a divorced couple wondering how to negotiate with your ex-spouse about planning a bar/bat mitzvah celebration.

  An interfaith family seriously considering the option of preparing your child or children for bar/bat mitzvah.

- Anyone with an interest in bar/bat mitzvah who wants to learn new perspectives and approaches to the ritual.

- Jewish educators working with b'nai mitzvah students who want to hear — and understand — the parents' perspective as well as learn from other colleagues' experience.

- Rabbis or cantors who want to gain new insights into families' priorities in preparing for bar/bat mitzvah.

ALSO BY CANTOR HELEN LENEMAN

Bar/Bat Mitzvah Education: A Sourcebook

Bar/Bat Mitzvah Basics

A Practical Family Guide to Coming of Age Together

EDITED BY
CANTOR
HELEN
LENEMAN

Jewish Lights Publishing
Woodstock, Vermont

Bar/Bat Mitzvah Basics: A Practical Family Guide to Coming of Age Together
© 1996 by Helen Leneman

Quote from Nancy Gad-Harf in Chapter 2 from *At 13, The Mitzvot: Family Resource Guide to Bar/Bat Mitzvah* (Farmington Hills, Mich.: Hillel Day School of Metropolitan Detroit, 1994). Reprinted by permission.

Portions of "Michael Becomes Bar Mitzvah: The Story of a Special Needs Child" by Beverly Weaver originally appeared in *United Synagogue Review*, Spring 1995. Reprinted by permission.

Parts of Rabbi Sandy Eisenberg Sasso's speeches to her children that appear in Chapter 13 were originally published in *Reconstructionist* magazine, vol. LV/No. 2, November/December 1989; and in the Foreword to *Putting God on the Guest List: How to Reclaim the Spiritual Meaning of Your Child's Bar or Bat Mitzvah* (Woodstock, Vt.: Jewish Lights Publishing, 1992). Reprinted by permission.

"The Bat Mitzvah Dress" by Nechama Liss-Levinson originally appeared in *Lilith* magazine, Fall 1994. Reprinted by permission.

Library of Congress Cataloging-in-Publication Data

Bar/Bat Mitzvah Basics: a practical family guide to coming of age together / edited by Helen Leneman.
   p.   cm.
   Includes bibliographical reference and index.
   ISBN 1-879045-51-6. — ISBN 1-879045-54-0 (pbk.)
   1. Bar mitzvah—Handbooks, manuals, etc. 2. Bat mitzvah—Handbooks, manuals, etc. I. Leneman, Helen.
   BM707.2.B369 1996
   296.4'424—dc20   96-1613
                                   CIP

10 9 8 7 6 5 4 3 2 1

ISBN 1-879045-51-6 (Hardcover)
ISBN 1-879045-54-0 (Quality Paperback)

Manufactured in the United States of America
Cover design: Donna Wohlfarth
Book design: Reuben Kantor

Published by Jewish Lights Publishing
A Division of LongHill Partners, Inc.
P.O. Box 237
Sunset Farm Offices, Rte. 4
Woodstock, Vermont 05091
Tel: (802) 457-4000   Fax: (802) 457-4004

DEDICATION

*To my father, David Leneman, of blessed memory, who
instilled in me an early love of Jewish learning*

*To Sima and Maya, who have inspired and
encouraged me in my life's work*

TABLE OF CONTENTS

Acknowledgments

I dedicate this book, above all, to you, the American Jewish family. You continue to invest time, energy, commitment, love, (and of course, money) to give your sons and daughters meaningful, memorable b'nai mitzvah celebrations. I deeply admire your sense of commitment and your many sacrifices, which stem from an attachment to our heritage and a love of Jewish traditions.

I salute my students and their parents — past, present and future — who are a constant source of inspiration. From my first bar mitzvah student in the summer of 1980 to the students of yesterday afternoon, I have watched as the revelation of Torah leads to other revelations: About self, about family, about community, about Judaism. As students internalize the Torah and Haftarah chant, they also internalize the eternal messages of these books. As the children change and grow, their families grow with them. Parents and children learn more than Jewish history and Bible: They also learn each others' and our communities' values. In addition, they discover what they are capable of accomplishing when there is emotional and intellectual investment and true commitment. Long before the *aliyah* to the Torah, family members have ascended to heights they never reached before.

In particular, I want to thank all those families that openly shared their experiences with me. You have done a great service, for by sharing your stories and insights, you are helping the families which follow you.

I also want to thank those who contributed essays or chapters that were not included in this book. All the material was absorbed and used in some fashion, and each piece became part of the whole.

Thank you to Rabbi Sandy Eisenberg Sasso who encouraged me to approach Jewish Lights Publishing with this book. She is a continued source of support and ideas.

Thank you to John Price, computer pro, who saved me countless hours of work by converting disk after disk to speed up the editing process.

A particular thank you to those families who gave most generously of their time to share their experiences with others: the Blacklow, Nearpass, Savage and White families. Thank you to Patti Weiner, director of Half-Pint Party Planners in Gaithersburg, Maryland for clarifying the functions of party planners.

The book could never have been finished without the constant editing, re-editing and final editing (and then, final final editing) of Arthur Magida, editorial director of Jewish Lights, who has taught me to hone, abbreviate, fine-tune and rein in my verbosity and metaphoric aspirations. And Stuart Matlins, Jewish Lights' publisher, who forced me to focus and zero in on my topics still further, and who saw the potential in my idea right from the start. His trust and support bolstered my faith in this book.

And I thank Sima — my personal editor, computer maven and constant source of support — who read every page, heard every story, and continually inspired me. This book is a tribute to the energizing effect you have on my life and work. Thank you for always being there.

FOREWORD

Rabbi Jeffrey K. Salkin
CENTRAL SYNAGOGUE OF NASSAU COUNTY, ROCKVILLE CENTRE, NEW YORK

"Spirituality" is an important focus among Jews today. Having written two books with "spirituality" in the title, I appreciate the need that we have for something deeper and higher, for that which can touch our souls in the holiest of places.

Over the past six years, I have spent much time thinking about spirituality. In *Putting God on the Guest List*, I sought to help parents recapture the spiritual aspects of American Jewry's most popular and least understood celebration — bar and bat mitzvah. The response to *Putting God on the Guest List: How to Reclaim the Spiritual Meaning of Your Child's Bar or Bat Mitzvah* has been gratifying. Rabbis and parents tell me that it has helped American Jews to think more seriously about bar and bat mitzvah and has prompted some to see the vast spiritual potential in this rite of passage: To acknowledge how a deepened sense of worship, Torah, mitzvah, and values can make the celebration into more than we had ever thought possible.

The need to write *Putting God on the Guest List* was clear. Most Jews understood that there was clearly more here than that which they were experiencing — and they wanted to experience it. I then decided to explore another area, one more difficult for most of us: The world of work, career and business. In *Being God's Partner: How to Find the Hidden Link Between Spirituality and Your Work*, I developed a theology of the workplace to help Jews and others see how even our mundane tasks could be elevated to the holy.

But throughout both of these books, and in day-to-day life as a congregational rabbi, I have learned something else that is equally valuable. When the prophet Ezekiel had a mystical vision of the divine beings, he noticed that each had not only wings that stretched to the heavens, but human hands under their wings (Ezekiel 1:8). Our spirituality must give us wings to ascend to the heights of existence, but we still need human hands to take care of the practical matters of existence. There must be a practical side to our spirituality. Just as the Torah describes the design of the desert tabernacle, its furnishings, and the priestly garments in exquisite detail, so, too, we learn every day: God is in the details. It is not enough merely to hope for the spiritual high of the great moments in life. We must "plan" those high moments, choreograph them — and yes, even manage them. That is why I was delighted when Cantor Helen Leneman decided to develop this book. I have known of Cantor Leneman's work for years. We have worked together on the B'nai Mitzvah Educators Network of the Coalition for the Advancement of Jewish Education. She is a committed educator. We are indebted to her for assembling a book that gathers so many practical bar and bat mitzvah-related details in one place. While my own book, *Putting God on the Guest List*, primarily addresses seeking *sanctity* in this rite of passage, I hope that parents will use *Bar/Bat Mitzvah Basics* as a way to find *sanity*.

Truth be told, bar/bat mitzvah celebration is virtually unique in modern Jewish history. Along with the observance of Hanukah, it is among the only Jewish observances that have actually *grown* in modern times and is more important now than it has ever been. We need to make sure that its *significance* keeps up with its *importance*. In my experience, much of the frenetic pre-bar or bat mitzvah activity has little or nothing to do with the *meaning* of the moment. Don't confuse this book with books that are only bar and bat mitzvah planners. *Bar/Bat Mitzvah Basics* goes far beyond the party aspects of bar/bat mitzvah. It helps us ponder the very impor-tant concept that the entire family is involved in the passage of bar/bat mitzvah. It helps the family of the bar/bat mitzvah teen see the event as an important moment in the entire family's emotional system and in which a host of "peripheral" issues have a way of becoming central.

Let us focus just briefly on one much-discussed and controversial aspect of the bar/bat mitzvah experience: The ethics of celebration. If anything shows how bar/bat mitzvah celebration has grown over the years, it is the entire nature of the party. What was once a sermonette delivered over a glass of *schnapps* and some herring on a *Shabbat* afternoon has expanded into a multi-million-dollar industry that includes party planners, disc jockeys and invitations made from space age materials or that are on video tape. Didn't the current generation of Jewish parents promise that we would reject the *Goodbye, Columbus* approach to celebration? Yet, the party hoopla around bar/bat mitzvah has often gotten out of hand. Our children — and Judaism — deserve something better.

Cantor Leneman's book will show you how bar/bat mitzvah can play an important role in your family's life. It will also help you survive this passage with graciousness, joy and good sense while you know that your child has just added his or her voice to the collective voice of generations — and that your child and you have done more than simply a "good job."

PREFACE

Rabbi Julie Gordon
TEMPLE OF AARON, ST. PAUL, MINNESOTA

I am writing this foreword minutes after concluding a meeting with parents of my congregation's sixth graders. They had gathered to discuss their sons' and daughters' upcoming bar and bat mitzvah celebrations. I heard their questions and I saw the anxiety on their faces. "There is so much to think about," remarked several parents. "I feel overwhelmed."

To which I replied, "Pick up the phone. Come in to see me or anyone else on our staff. We are here to help you make this life cycle celebration meaningful and memorable."

How I wish I could have given them this book to ease their anxiety. I am confident that, in the future, parents whose child is about to become a bar or bat mitzvah will find *Bar/Bat Mitzvah Basics* to be of great assistance.

We are indebted to Cantor Helen Leneman for bringing together the programs, ideas and honesty of the rabbis, cantors, therapists, educators, parents and teens who contributed to this book. In fact, *Bar/Bat Mitzvah Basics* reminds me of *The Jewish Catalog*, the beloved collection that taught Jewish tradition in a new way for a new generation back in the 1970s. As with *The Jewish Catalog*, we can gain a great deal of insight from *Bar/Bat Mitzvah Basics* whether we read it from cover to cover or pick and choose from those chapters that are most relevant to our individual circumstances.

Bar/Bat Mitzvah Basics is especially needed at this moment in the history of American Jewry since it weaves together the thinking and the experience of many in the Jewish community regarding bar and bat mitzvah. This is an era in which our communities, our faith, our families and sometimes even we ourselves are fragmented and disjointed. It is an era in which we can vastly benefit from each other's wisdom, a time in which we should rely much more than we usually do on the advice encapsulated in this phrase that is said upon concluding a book of the Torah: *"Hazak hazak ve-nit-ha-zayk,"* "Be strong and together may we strengthen each other."

Bar/Bat Mitzvah Basics can help us rethink our commitment to Jewish identity and Jewish education. It can especially help us to resolve the very fundamental, sometimes very vexing issues that are inherent in bar and bat mitzvah preparation: Working with rabbis, clergy and educators; planning a creative service that is appropriate to your family; deciding whom to invite to the celebration; even deciding the words that might be on invitations for the bar or bat mitzvah of a child who does not have a "traditional" family con-stellation. These may be the "mechanics" of a bar or bat mitzvah, but they are also what give so many parents (and their children) the jitters about this event that has the potential to be so meaningful to them.

We will be wiser after reading *Bar/Bat Mitzvah Basics* — and after learning from it. May it inspire us to celebrate our children becoming b'nai mitzvah with greater sanity, less anxiety and with greater commitment to God, Torah and our people.

INTRODUCTION

Cantor Helen Leneman

Bar/Bat Mitzvah Basics focuses on the bar/bat mitzvah ceremony and celebration as the entire family's rite of passage and how they can bring about family growth. Written for families with upcoming b'nai mitzvah celebrations, it includes information and advice from everyone involved in the process — rabbis, cantors, religious school principals, tutors, psychologists and social workers — and accounts of bar/bat mitzvah experiences and important lessons learned from parents and post-b'nai mitzvah teens.

As a cantor and a bar/bat mitzvah educator, I have become aware of a need to better understand the potential of bar/bat mitzvah preparation for the spiritual and emotional growth of the entire family, not just the bar or bat mitzvah child.

With that in mind, this book addresses how to approach and successfully manage the bar/bat mitzvah process as an interfaith family; as a divorced parent; as the parent of a special needs child; and whether or not you are now affiliated with a synagogue. Also included are suggestions about how to design a creative service; what to say to your child on the *bimah*; and how to best utilize the resources provided by your congregation or local Jewish community. This includes advice on asking the right questions about bar/bat mitzvah education and preparation and informing yourself of all available options. Empowered with this increased understanding, you will be better able to harness the enormous potential for growth that the bar/bat mitzvah holds, both for children becoming b'nai mitzvah and for their families.

Each adult contributor to *Bar/Bat Mitzvah Basics* is a parent, and each is writing *as* a parent, even those who are synagogue or Jewish education professionals. They know the anxieties and worries of the mother or father of a bar or bat mitzvah, and how overwhelming the bar/bat mitzvah experience may seem. But they also know how special it can be. And they would like to help guide you through the thicket of your concerns so you can appreciate the experience for what it is: An opportunity for your entire family to experience the "high" of a very special day and to all embrace Torah, tradition, the Jewish community, and each other.

BAR/BAT MITZVAH IS JUST ONE PART OF A LIFETIME OF JEWISH LEARNING AND EXPERIENCE

Traditionally, the Jewish way of life has had its place in both the home and the congregation. The sages, in fact, applied Ezekiel's phrase, *mikdash meyat*, a "minor sanctuary," to both of these. The home has been the hub of such family-oriented rituals as lighting the *Shabbat* and Hanukah candles, maintaining the sanctity of the laws of *kashrut*, and feasting in a *sukkah* or celebrating at the Passover *seder* table. The congregation has been the hub of communal worship and scholarship and a sense of peoplehood in its broadest sense.

But recent years have seen an increase in the numbers of American Jews who are not affiliated with any congregation. According to the National Jewish Population Survey, for instance, the number of unaffiliated Jews increased by about 112,000 persons, or by 15 percent, in the two decades before 1990.

This situation must be faced honestly and frankly. So, too, must the unfortunate fact be faced that many parents do not even consider joining a congregation until their children approach the age of bar or bat mitzvah. They often do not understand the rich experiences that await them as a family that actively participates in the life of a vibrant congregation. They do not see bar/bat mitzvah as part of a lifelong process of Jewish learning.

Bar/Bat Mitzvah Basics recognizes these realities, even though it does not endorse them. But only by confronting them can the organized Jewish community begin to make the currently unaffiliated feel at home, and help them see the reasons for and the benefit of congregational affiliation.

BAR MITZVAH IS NOT WHAT YOU HAVE, IT IS WHAT YOU BECOME

Since we use language to express how we feel about things, the use — or misuse — of it can color our views. Therefore, it is critical that the reader properly understand the terminology used in discussing bar/bat mitzvah. Bar/bat mitzvah is often used as a verb (as in "bar or bat mitzvah-ed.") But bar mitzvah actually means "son of, or subject to, the commandment," which means that one doesn't have a bar or bat mitzvah. Instead, one *becomes* bar or bat mitzvah. Using the term properly helps us recognize the act of becoming. To *have* a bar/bat mitzvah would put the special day in a single moment in time only, with a focus on the celebration or party. This diminishes the act of becoming.

"Bar" is the Aramaic word for "son" as well as an idiom for "subject to." Aramaic was spoken in Babylon, where the Jewish people lived in exile beginning in the sixth century B.C.E. after the destruction of the first temple in Jerusalem. Aramaic also was spoken in Israel. Much of the Talmud (the teachings and commentary on the Torah written between 200 and 500 C.E.) was written in Aramaic, and the first mention of bar mitzvah dates to the Talmudic period.

"Bat" is Hebrew for daughter. Hebrew is used rather than Aramaic because the ceremony for girls began in 1922, when Rabbi Mordecai Kaplan, founder of Reconstructionist Judaism, decided a religious coming-of-age ceremony for his daughter, Judith, was appropriate. Some people say "bas mitzvah," "bas" being the Ashkenazi or Eastern European pronunciation of "bat." "Bat" is the Sephardic pronunciation, which is used in contemporary Israeli Hebrew.

The term "b'nai mitzvah" is used throughout this book. Children become "b'nai mitzvah" at a bar or bat mitzvah service, ceremony or celebration. "B'nai," which is a plural possessive meaning "sons or children of," is interchangeable in this book with bar/bat mitzvah. Neither "bar mitzvahs" nor "b'nai mitzvot" is a correct term. Though "mitzvot" is the plural of "mitzvah," "mitz-vah" remains the same whether preceded by a singular form like "bar" or the plural "b'nai." (You might think of this as you would think of both of your *mothers*-in-law; while tempting, it is incorrect grammatically to say "*mother*-in-laws.)

When a boy or girl *becomes* bar or bat mitzvah, he or she becomes responsible for the Jewish laws and precepts pertaining to adult Jews. Every Jewish child automatically becomes bar or bat mitzvah, with or without a ceremony. According to tradition, a girl becomes bat mitzvah at age 12, and a boy becomes bar mitzvah at age 13. The Bible doesn't mention either bar (or bat) mitzvah or the age of 13, but the Talmud states that at the age of 13 a boy is subject to the commandments.

The concept of the bar/bat mitzvah ceremony as we know it today probably started between the 14th and 16th centuries in Germany and Poland. The ceremony was held at a regular *Shabbat* morning service, during which the boy who had recently turned 13 would display his knowledge and be honored by being called up for an *aliyah*.

The essential meaning of bar and bat mitzvah is that it is a milestone, not an end, of Jewish study and identity. In a famous *midrash*, or rabbinic legend, Abraham smashed his father's idols when he was 13, therefore becoming the first Jew. Each bar or bat mitzvah ceremony can be considered a symbolic rebirth of Judaism, the creation of a new Jewish soul with its promise yet to be realized: The ceremony celebrates the act of becoming, which is, of course, a life-long process.

The custom of an *aliyah*, being called up to the Torah to say blessings before and after a reading, probably began in the first century C.E. The blessings we say today for an *aliyah* are probably the same ones used then. Reciting them has become a symbol of the bar or bat mitzvah's acceptance of adult Jewish responsibilities. The first "*aliyah*" occurred when Moses ascended Mt. Sinai to receive the Torah. Connecting that event to the bar or bat mitzvah's first *aliyah* elevates all of the child's hard work preparing for this day to the act of becoming a full member of the Jewish community, part of a chain of generations that is thousands of years long.

Like our ancestors who stood at the threshold of the Promised Land, b'nai mitzvah who embrace the Jewish commandments do not necessarily understand all these commandments. But they are about to cross a threshold into young adulthood, and affirming the faith of their ancestors will surely guide them in that new territory.

WHAT'S BAR/BAT MITZVAH ALL ABOUT?

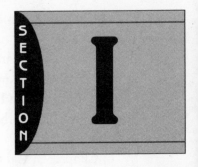

INTRODUCTION

Families who think there is only one approach to bar/bat mitzvah preparation or are reluctant or even afraid to ask questions of professionals in their congregation will learn in this section that there are many ways to approach bar/bat mitzvah education and preparation.

To let parents hear from a broad range of Jewish professionals, these seven chapters include the voices of rabbis, cantors and educators. They will help orient you to the fundamentals of bar and bat mitzvah, from the pragmatics of preparation to the spirituality and the magic of its broadest, deepest dimension.

In Chapter 1, Cantor Helen Leneman of Rockville, Maryland covers the basic elements of planning a bar or bat mitzvah celebration: Identifying a congregation you might like to join; choosing the date; understanding your child's tutoring schedule; and thinking about some of the deeper meanings of this event for your whole family. In addition, she explains how studying Torah as a family can enrich your bar/bat mitzvah experience, and shows how to go about it.

In Chapter 2, Susie Tatarka, education director of Adath Jeshurun Synagogue in St. Louis Park, Minnesota, gives concise, practical advice to parents looking ahead to b'nai mitzvah ceremonies for their children. In addition to directing the *Shabbat* morning program and Sunday religious school at Adath Jeshurun, Tatarka also directs the congregation's infant, toddler, daycare and preschool programs.

In Chapter 3, Cantor Marshall Portnoy of Main Line Reform Temple in Wynnewood, Pennsylvania, helps parents understand themselves and their expectations for their children's b'nai mitzvah celebrations. From his many years of preparing b'nai mitzvah children and their parents, Cantor Portnoy suggests some major ingredients for a successful process.

Chapter 4, also by Cantor Leneman, is a guide designed to empower you as parents to ask the right questions about your children's bar/bat mitzvah preparation, by explaining the key elements involved in the bar/bat mitzvah education process. With improved understanding, you will be better able to help your children study and learn.

In Chapter 5, Rabbi Susan B. Stone of Temple Beth Shalom in Hudson, Ohio, helps you understand how the bar/bat mitzvah is a rite of passage as much for yourself as for your children. She suggests ways for you to increase your involvement in your congregation's community.

In Chapter 6, Dr. Judith Davis, a licensed family therapist who teaches at the University of Massachusetts and practices in Amherst, discusses how viewing the bar/bat mitzvah as a true ritual, filled with drama and magic, can offer families new insights and meaning for the whole experience.

In Chapter 7, Rabbi Jeffrey K. Salkin of Central Synagogue in Rockville Centre, New York, points out how bar/bat mitzvah preparation often brings long-buried religious ambivalence to the surface of some parents' minds and suggests ways to settle doubts.

Bar/Bat Mitzvah Basic Elements

Start to Finish

Cantor Helen Leneman

Your child is about to turn 11 and you suddenly realize that his or her bar or bat mitzvah celebration is only two years away. How do you start planning for that event? If you are affiliated with a congregation, it will provide guidelines and meetings with its staff, so there is no need for you to panic. Yet, it is still best to be as informed as possible from the outset. If you are not already affiliated with a congregation and you would like to join one, consider the following ways to get information about congregations which might be best for you, bearing in mind that there are four main branches of Judaism in the United States: Reform, Reconstructionist, Conservative and Orthodox. Also, a small but growing number of congregations are calling themselves "unaffiliated," "independent," or "post-denominational." These invariably fall within the liberal end of Judaism's theological spectrum.

- Consult the listing of local congregations in your Yellow Pages. These are usually under the heading of "synagogues."
- Ask friends about the congregations where they are affiliated. What sort of people belong (what are the demographics of the congregation)? What is the balance in the congregation between tradition and innovation? How is the congregation organized: Is it lay-oriented or rabbi-oriented? How do the rabbi(s), cantor(s),

educator(s), b'nai mitzvah tutors and other staff relate to and interact with the members? And most importantly for your present concerns, have any of your friends' children become bar or bat mitzvah at the congregation to which they presently belong — and how do they feel about that experience?

• If you cannot locate a congregation near you or those that you do know about do not appeal to you, write or call the following central offices of Judaism's denominational branches, asking for a listing of congregations in your immediate area. Perhaps also request pamphlets describing that denomination's core beliefs and practices:

Union of American Hebrew Congregations (UAHC) — Reform
838 Fifth Avenue
New York, NY 10021
(212) 249-0100

United Synagogue of Conservative Judaism
155 Fifth Avenue
New York, NY 10010
(212) 533-7800

The Jewish Reconstructionist Federation
Church Road and Greenwood Avenue
Wyncote, PA 19095
(215) 887-1988

Union of Orthodox Jewish Congregations
333 7th Avenue
New York, NY 10001
(212) 563-4000

Be assured that you will be warmly greeted in any congregation, as a visitor, as a potential member and as a fellow Jew. Do not be overly concerned about the financial aspects of joining a congregation since congregations typically make special provisions for potential members who lack the means to pay the congregation's full dues.

If you are not already affiliated with a congregation and decide not to join one, call your local Board of Jewish Education or Jewish Community Center for a list of b'nai mitzvah tutors whom you can hire to prepare your child for the bar/bat mitzvah service and/or a list of Hebrew schools in your area that are independent of congregations and in which you can enroll your son or daughter.

CHOOSING THE DATE — THE KEY ISSUES TO CONSIDER

One of the first decisions you will face regarding your child's bar or bat mitzvah ceremony is choosing a date. Not all congregations give you much choice, but you should be aware of several factors.

Constraints of the Congregation's Calendar

A boy becomes bar mitzvah on his 13th birthday; a girl becomes bat mitzvah on her 12th birthday. But not every congregation or denomination adheres to that rule; many insist the ceremony be held after the 13th birthday for both girls and boys. It is Jewish tradition to hold the bar or bat mitzvah ceremony on the *Shabbat* closest to the birthday. In many large congregations, it is not possible to accommodate each family this way. In general, most families prefer to hold the ceremony within a month or two of the birthday.

Constraints of Climate and Weather

If you are given a choice of dates, weigh all the pros and cons of each. The winter months are fine for mild climates, but much less desirable for harsher climates. Blizzards in the snowbelt have postponed many a bar/bat mitzvah ceremony. Snowbirds vacationing in Florida will often attend *Shabbat* services at the local congregation. This may bring overflow crowds to the sanctuary on the *Shabbat* of your child's service. Summer is the least popular time because so many children and their friends are on vacation. Therefore, fall and spring dates are overcrowded and hardest to obtain in large congregations.

CONTENT OF THE TORAH PORTION

The time of year you choose will also determine the content of your child's Torah portion. The Five Books of Moses are read in sequence every year: The 54 weekly portions are read in most years in a 52-week cycle. Since the Jewish calendar is lunar and the civil calendar is solar, there is fluctuation of about a month in the following outline: Reading Genesis starts right after the High Holy Days, which occur in September or October; Exodus usually starts some time in January; Leviticus in March; Numbers in May; Deuteronomy in July. The most interesting, well-known "stories" are in Genesis and Exodus. Leviticus and Deuteronomy have large sections that resemble legal treatises.

A good teacher, of course, can always extract nuggets from any Torah portion to capture a student's imagination. But if you have a choice, check a Jewish calendar for the weekly portions listed on the dates you are considering. To determine a reading two years or more in advance, consult a perpetual Jewish calendar. If you are doing this only one year in advance, each portion is listed on most one-year Jewish calendars under the Hebrew date. You can find the portion (*parasha*) in a *chumash* (which contains the Five Books of Moses, also known as the Torah) and consider its content when deciding on the bar/bat mitzvah date.

Remember that your child will probably only read a part of the weekly portion: In some Conservative congregations, the bar/bat mitzvah reads only the *maftir* portion, the concluding verses of the Torah portion; in others, the child will read the *entire* portion, sometimes over 100 verses. In most Reform and Reconstructionist, and some Conservative congregations, the bar/bat mitzvah reads between 10 and 30 verses of the Torah portion. Some families choose the same portion that one of the child's parents read at his or bar or bat mitzvah ceremony. I once taught a girl who used her father's own "Bar Mitzvah Booklet" which he had kept for over 25 years.

The bar or bat mitzvah generally will also read a *Haftarah* portion, a selection from the Prophets, the second book of the *Tanach* or Hebrew Bible. Specific readings from the Prophets were chosen by the rabbis many centuries ago, to correspond in some way to the ideas of the Torah portion of the week.

Enriching Family Life Through Torah Study

Since a bar or bat mitzvah celebration is part of a process, not an isolated event, the year leading up to the ceremony can be seen as an opportunity for the family to learn, experience and grow together. There are three "academic" areas in which learning and growth can take place: Torah, Hebrew and the *Shabbat* liturgy.

Studying Torah together as a family has the potential for great enrichment. Establish realistic goals regarding how much and how often to study together. The key is to establish a *set time* for Torah study — and then to stick to it.

Many families will set aside time at the *Shabbat* dinner table for Torah discussions. The content and quality of these discussions count far more than the frequency. While some congregations help several families get together for evenings of Torah study, either on Friday evening or another week night, you can coordinate such evenings yourself with other families.

Do not feel overwhelmed by the expression "Torah study." Start simply, with your child's assigned Torah portion, and determine its:

Context: In which biblical book is the portion found? What is the broad outline of that book? What happens before and after this particular portion?

Content: What is this portion about? What happens? Why? How? What is the result?

Meaning: What is the message to be gleaned from the events in this portion that may be relevant to us today? Is there a particularly meaningful, or even disturbing, element that you want to focus on?

Numerous resources can guide you in this study. (See "Selected Resources for Parents," Appendix A.) By studying Torah together as a Jewish family, you will be wonderful role models for your children. You will also establish new, meaningful relationships with them, with your study partners, with the Torah and with your Jewish heritage and community. As Dr. Nancy Gad-Harf, program and development director at Temple Israel, a Reform congregation in West Bloomfield, Michigan, wrote in *At 13, The Mitzvot: Family Resource Guide to Bar/Bat Mitzvah*,

> The process of becoming a bar or bat mitzvah can be used by the entire family to grow, to think, and to live Jewishly. How many of us know our child's Torah portion as well as we know the comparative costs of bands, caterers, and party-planners? How many of us spend as much time studying our child's *Haftarah* as we do on finding clothes for the party?
>
> If we begin to think of our child as "becoming" (rather than "having") a bar or bat mitzvah, we can begin to build Jewish experiences around it, experiences that will create a lifetime of Jewish memories that will last long after we have forgotten the theme of our party.
>
> How does a family accomplish this goal? First, understand that the actual ceremony is just one Jewish life cycle

event in a continuum of many. It is neither a starting nor a finishing point. If a child only learns to memorize a Torah portion with its accompanying *Haftarah* and only donates money to a worthy cause (usually by way of a tax-deductible check written by the parents), that child loses the context in which the bar or bat mitzvah ceremony has any significance at all. So, too, do his or her parents and siblings.

On the other hand, if a family begins to study the Torah portion together well in advance of the ceremony and identifies hands-on *tzedakah* projects, it can begin to understand the significance of the bar/bat mitzvah process: Becoming responsible as an adult member of the Jewish community. An 11- or 12-year old child cannot usually do this alone. He or she needs the support and guidance of parents. As parents, then, we must re-order our priorities. We must take the time to study the Torah, to find and participate in social action projects, to attend *Shabbat* services and observe *Shabbat* as an integral part of our lives.

TIME OF THE SERVICE

Another decision concerns the *time* of the service. While a *Shabbat* morning service, of course, is the most common setting for a bar or bat mitzvah ceremony, it is not the only time that you can have the ceremony:

- *Havdalah* services have become increasingly popular. The *Havdalah* ceremony, which is traditionally done in the home at the end of *Shabbat*, marks the separation between *Shabbat* and the weekdays that follow it. Blessings are said over a special braided candle, over sweet spices, and over wine.

- A late Saturday afternoon or early evening bar or bat mitzvah service can incorporate elements of the traditional *mincha/ma'ariv* (afternoon/evening) service, which contains many of the same prayers as the *Shabbat* morning service and includes a Torah reading, but not a *Haftarah* reading.
- Friday evening, when the Torah is read in some Reform congregations.
- Monday or Thursday morning, when the Torah is read in Orthodox congregations, in many Conservative congregations and in some Reform congregations.
- The Torah is also read on Rosh Chodesh (the new moon) and such festivals as Pesach or Sukkot. The holiday might even be the theme of your celebration.

ONE YEAR AND COUNTING — MAJOR STEPS IN PLANNING FOR THE SERVICE AND CELEBRATION

The Place

Now that you have the date, you need everything else! Reserving a place for the party is usually done at least a year in advance. You can make all the party arrangements yourself, or you can hire a "party planner" who will do most of the planning for you. (More about this in Chapter 18, which discusses the role of a party planner.)

Studying

Many congregations begin holding meetings with the b'nai mitzvah family at least a year before the date of their celebration. Private tutoring for bar/bat mitzvah students might start as late as six to as early as twelve months before the bar/bat mitzvah date.

You should make arrangements with the tutor several months in advance of this time, and ask about his or her timetable.

Below is an example of a six-month schedule and what might take place at each stage. It should be noted that half a year is the minimum for tutoring and that each congregation and denominational movement has its own standards and criteria for bar and bat mitzvah.

For example, the Conservative movement places greater emphasis on the *Haftarah* than on the Torah portion; therefore, the order in which these two are learned might be reversed in the timetable below.

MONTH 1

- The student might learn *trope*, or cantillation, a system of symbols enabling him or her to "de-code" and chant his or her own *Haftarah* and/or Torah portion. Many Reform and Conservative cantors offer classes in *trope*.
- The Torah portion is read and discussed at home by the whole family. A section of greatest interest to the student is chosen; the number of verses may depend on your congregation's custom, as well as on the number of *aliyot* (family members or special family friends honored with an *aliyah* — being called up to say a blessing before and after each section of the reading). At a minimum, in most congregations, the bar or bat mitzvah has an *aliyah*, as do parents, grandparents and, in most cases, siblings over age 13. A minimum of three verses, and often more, is read for each *aliyah*. But this is not always the case.

MONTHS 2–3

- The Torah portion is learned in private lessons and, in addition, with an audiotape of the portion that is listened to at home for practice. It is learned verse by verse, first with and later without vowels.
- The student begins to write an introduction to the Torah portion which will be read aloud to the congregation at the bar/bat mitzvah service. Writing this encourages the student to read traditional and modern commentaries on the portion and develop his or her own interpretation of it.

MONTHS 4–5

- For *Shabbat* morning services, a different system of trope for the *Haftarah* reading (a selection from the Book of Prophets), is learned.
- The *Haftarah* portion and its blessings are learned.
- For *Havdalah* services, a longer Torah reading is learned, followed by *Havdalah* service prayers.

MONTH 6

- For *Shabbat* morning services, the student may write an introduction to his/her *Haftarah* portion, which will be read at the service. This helps students learn the historical context of their particular reading and why the early rabbis chose it to be read after a particular Torah portion.
- Prayers not already learned in Hebrew school will be learned for the service, and prayers the student knows will be thoroughly reviewed. For *Havdalah*, special prayers will be learned.
- A complete run-through, with the Torah scroll, will be held, usually in the sanctuary, with the rabbi, cantor or b'nai mitzvah teacher. Questions about who will do what, the choreography and order of the service will be answered at this session, or at a later session closer to the date, with the student and his or her family.

The Guest List

As soon as you pick the bar/bat mitzvah date, it is a good idea to inform those family members and friends who you want to be sure are with you at this special time, so that they can plan ahead comfortably.

At least three months before the ceremony, your family should compile a guest list. This chore often involves much negotiation between family members, over such issues as the maximum number of guests you want to include, how many of these should be your child's friends, and how many your friends and business associates; and whether or not to invite distant relatives with whom you have lost contact over the years. It is wise to have a short "alternate" list of people you deem less essential, but would still like to have at the ceremony. That way, as RSVP's come in, you can fill vacancies from your list of "alternate choices." Formal invitations are usually sent six to eight weeks before the ceremony.

THE SPIRITUAL AND EMOTIONAL MEANING

Do not let the technical matters overshadow the deeper spiritual and religious meanings of this year of preparation for your family. As Dr. Helene Kalson Cohen, assistant principal of the Hillel Day School of Metropolitan Detroit, has written: "The 12- or 13-year-old is going through major changes: Physical, social, emotional, intellectual and moral. These children wake up month after month to find that their bodies are changing. It's twenty minutes before their Hebrew school carpool is scheduled to arrive, and the dress that fit last month no longer fits...They look in the mirror and see their complexion is changing...Their friends look different. The boys' voices are deeper. Friends that they used to look down at, now tower over them...Social groups form and dissolve and re-form...Mood swings catch children and parents by surprise...As our children's intellectual capacities solidify, so does their ability to mount a complicated, compelling argument...Our child's moral reasoning is also developing. There is now the potential for a new sense of justice and caring to emerge."

As you begin planning the bar/bat mitzvah ceremony, remember to pay attention to the extraordinary, powerful ways that your child is changing before your eyes. You also might begin to notice changes within your entire family, as all of you move together towards this rite of passage.

WHAT PARENTS SHOULD KNOW *BEFORE* THE BAR/BAT MITZVAH CEREMONY

Susie Tatarka

As education director for a large Conservative congregation in the Midwest, I come into contact with all our families before their child's bar/bat mitzvah services. They all know that this is an important event in their family's life, but for some families it becomes a life-changing event, a chance to reconnect with their families' traditions, to study Jewish texts, to feel they are a link in a long chain that goes back into Jewish history and forward into a Jewish future. Those are the fortunate ones who have meaningful ceremonies that uplift all of us who are present on the *Shabbat* morning of their child's ceremony.

Here are some factors that enable families to truly make their bar/bat mitzvah ceremonies memorable that should be thought about in the year or two before the bar/bat mitzvah date.

PREPARE FOR THE FUTURE

Be aware that your family will have to make an emotional and spiritual "investment" for this event to be truly memorable.

You have to be willing to really think about how you and your family are living your lives. Do you like where your Jewish choices have taken you? Are you comfortable with your present level of Jewish observance? Thirteen years ago, at your child's *brit milah* or baby naming, you probably, as have countless Jewish parents over the generations, hoped that just as he or she has entered the *brit* (covenant), so may he or she continue to study Torah, to have a Jewish wedding and a life of *Maasim Tovim* (a "life of good deeds").

The bar/bat mitzvah is almost a mid-point stop in the journey you take with your child. At the birth, you were full of hopes and dreams. The whole future lay before you like a blank sheet waiting to be written on. By now, you have shared about 12 years of family life and you can look back — and forward. This is a good time to make a mid-journey evaluation and, if necessary, to reset the compass. By now, you have learned that children learn more from what we do than from what we say.

First, look at your home life. As Rabbi Abraham Joshua Heschel said, "A Jewish home is a home where Judaism is at home." Does this describe your house? If not, take steps to change things. You might find that there are families in your community who would love to join in a *havurah* (Jewish fellowship group) that would meet once a month and celebrate *Shabbat* together.

Or, if you are not comfortable with *Shabbat* and holiday rituals and would like to learn more about them, there are many books and workshops that you could learn from. You will be surprised by how enriched your family life might become when you make your home a *mikdash meyat*, a small temple, a sacred place.

You are about to bring your child to Torah and *Maasim Tovim*. Think about the place these have in your life. Does your child see you give to charity? Or study Jewish texts? Or perform deeds of loving kindness? In what ways have you ensured, as much as today's parent can, that your child will want to continue to live a Jewish life after leaving your home? Have you helped your child form Jewish connections by sending him or her to a Jewish school? Are summers spent in a Jewish camp?

A connection to Israel can also be a very important part of your child's Jewish identity. You can start planning for a family trip or your child's trip to Israel as part of the bar/bat mitzvah preparations. Jack Moline, a Conservative rabbi in Alexandria, Virginia, says that among the many things that parents don't say enough to their children is: "You have a home in Israel." That is a powerful message to send to your child. Israel is central to Jewish history. Traveling there is a life-changing event for many Jews. Many Jewish communities have funds to help parents send their children to Israel after their bar/bat mitzvah ceremony. This is certainly worth inquiring about, either at your congregation or local Board of Jewish Education.

ATTEND SYNAGOGUE REGULARLY

Be familiar with the liturgy of the Shabbat service and be able to participate in it so it is meaningful to you.

I have attended a few bar/bat mitzvah ceremonies where the families seemed totally uncomfortable with the ritual. They were not certain when to stand, what they were supposed to do and even where they should sit. I felt sad for them. On this day, which should be one of the happiest in their lives, all they felt was anxiety and tension.

By attending *Shabbat* services regularly, you will feel comfortable and familiar with the different parts of the service. Many parents tell me that attending services for at least six months before the bar/bat mitzvah ceremony made them appreciate the many skills their child was learning and made them want to learn more about their traditions. Think how your child would feel if his or her learning inspired you to learn more. Think of the thrill for him or her to be able to teach *you* something for a change! Parents who have done this tell me that they experienced a new connection to their child.

EXPERIENCE COMMUNITY

Feel a connection with the congregation that will celebrate your child's bar/bat mitzvah ceremony with you.

Regularly attending *Shabbat* services means that by the time your bar/bat mitzvah day comes, you will probably have friends at the congregation whom you might not have known or been close to before. You might, by finding parents whose children are the same age as yours, create a supportive group of like-minded friends for yourself. Families in my community have joined together to help each other with different aspects of their bar/bat mitzvah celebrations, such as transporting out-of-town guests to and from the airport, sponsoring a Sunday brunch for these guests, or baking for each others' *Shabbat Kiddush*. It is wonderful to be a part of a community that together celebrates happy, as well as sad occasions.

A mother once told me she resented that, in the middle of the *Shabbat* service for her son's bar mitzvah ceremony, the rabbi "spoiled" their joy by mentioning congregants who were in the hospital. Even worse, he mentioned who had died that week. "It really put a damper on our *simcha*," she said. After my initial anger at her passed, I realized that she had felt this way because she and her husband had never tried to make themselves part of the community and didn't understand what community is all about. I felt sad for them.

Your child should feel that becoming a Jewish adult means joining a vibrant, loving community that will be happy when your child celebrates and will offer support when he or she mourns. That is what being part of a congregation is all about and what you, as a Jewish parent, should teach to your child. One of my children's most memorable Jewish experiences was the week I sat *shiva* in our home. They learned what a community is about and how everyone can come together and help the family through a difficult time.

TRUST YOUR CHILD

Be confident about your child's level of competence and preparedness.

One aspect of the preparation that I emphasize is that, if the bar/bat mitzvah is to mean anything in terms of learning to be responsible for oneself, it is imperative that the student be accountable for the training. We may give a student additional help during the week if needed, or arrange for tutors who can call during the week to listen to a student's progress over the phone. (For parents' convenience, many of our tutorials are done over the phone.) But in the final analysis, no one can study for the student. Only the student can do it. We recommend that students study approximately half an hour twice a day in the six months immediately before their b'nai mitzvah service. Some students need less; some need more. I tell students that their preparation and study will be a valuable experience that they can use for the rest of their life. Whenever they are faced with an enormous task, all they will have to do is remember how enormous the task of preparing for their bar/bat mitzvah service seemed to be — and how, by breaking the task down into manageable goals, they completed all the work.

It might be difficult for you, as parents, to leave the responsibility in the hands of your child. Some parents nag their child incessantly, creating tension over what should be a joyous occasion. I have found that when the parents convey the message that they trust their child to do what is needed to fulfill their responsibilities, then the child "worries" instead of the parent — and does what needs to be done.

REMEMBER THE SPIRITUAL

Carefully plan the event, but keep in mind what is really important.

A friend once told me after her child's bar mitzvah service that she wished she had thought as much about what she was going to say to her son on the *bimah* as she had about planning the menu. It is easy to get caught up in the social planning and the minor details. I attend about forty bar/bat mitzvah events a year, but I don't recollect the menu at any of them. What I do remember are moments of incredible warmth when parents gave their child a *tallit* that had belonged to a beloved grandparent, when a grandfather spoke eloquently of becoming bar mitzvah in Poland just before the Holocaust, and when various family members read from the Torah. Such moments make you think, "God *is* in this place."

Remember that this is a milestone in the life of your child and your family. Don't get so bogged down in the social details that you forget the spiritual. How you commemorate this event sends an important message to your child as she or he becomes an adult Jew. Focusing on planning the menu without giving *tzedakah* to feed the hungry tells your child about your priorities. Use this special time to teach your child what living a Jewish life means to you and your family. In this way, your child's becoming bar or bat mitzvah will be what it was meant to be: The beginning of an adult Jewish life.

"Passing" the Bar (or Bat) Mitzvah

Setting Clear and Realistic Expectations for Everyone

Cantor Marshall Portnoy

Some parents who have planned a bar/bat mitzvah celebration may say it was one of their most delightful, fulfilling and bonding experiences. Or they may say they couldn't wait for the Monday after the bar/bat mitzvah ceremony, when the whole pressured mess (except the bills) was behind them. Most parents will probably express elation *and* relief. There are ways to experience more of the former and less of the latter.

Bar/bat mitzvah can be an opportunity for young people to deepen their fluency in Hebrew, to better understand Jewish prayer, to intensify their Jewish identity. It can help them connect to their own family and to the values that have shaped the Jewish people from ancient days to the present. Above all, it can enhance self-confidence and self-respect and affirm one's worth and talents. Yet, the experience sometimes falls short of this.

Assess Your Bar/Bat Mitzvah Expectations

At the outset, we should ask ourselves what we hope to get out of this experience. Below are six "expectations" that may be associated with your child's bar/bat mitzvah. Assign a number to each to indicate to what extent you agree with the statement:

---

5 Agree strongly
4 Agree somewhat
3 Neutral
2 Disagree somewhat
1 Disagree strongly

I view the bar/bat mitzvah as an opportunity to:

1. Help my child develop a positive Jewish identity and a genuine connection to his/her Jewish past, present and future:_____
2. See relatives and friends I haven't seen in a long time:_____
3. Give my child synagogue skills he/she can use for years afterwards:_____
4. Repay social obligations:_____
5. Deepen my family's commitment to Jewish values and a Jewish way of life:_____
6. Have a great time!:_____

Statements 1, 3 and 5 relate to the religious dimensions of the bar/bat mitzvah. If you scored a total of 12 or more points for these three items, you view the bar/bat mitzvah as an opportunity to intensify your family's religious involvement through preparation for the ceremony. Statements 2, 4 and 6 relate to the ceremony's social opportunities. Twelve or more total points on these items indicates that you view the ceremony as an opportunity to connect with people who are important to you.

From the standpoint of Jewish history and tradition, these two aspects — religious and community — are inextricable, since religious life and social life are bound together. Indeed, bar/bat mitz-vah is a declaration by the community that a young person has achieved a degree of maturity. It is marked by the young person's demonstration of religious skills, but it is not conducted in a school or office. It is celebrated in a *beit knesset*, a house of gathering. It is therefore appropriate to be concerned with both the religious and social aspects of this special day.

ASSESS WHERE YOU ARE NOW

Having considered what we would like the bar/bat mitzvah experience to bring to us, let's assess how we stand right now in some of these same areas by scoring the following statements as you did with those above, on a 1 to 5 continuum:

1. My child is proud to be a Jew and cares about broadening his/her understanding of his/her Jewish heritage:____
2. Keeping up with distant relatives and friends by telephone, letter (and e-mail!) is important to me:____
3. Seeing my child participate in formal Jewish life is extremely important to me:____
4. I feel a healthy sense of reciprocation, of "give and take," with friends, acquaintances and colleagues:____
5. My family's life is imbued with Jewish practices and Jewish values:____
6. I find it easy to have a great time:____

Record the scores from both sets of questions on this chart. Write down the answers to the first set of questions under column A, and the answers to the second set of questions under column B.

	A. What I'd Like	B. What I'm Like
Questions:	(#)	(#)
1. Jewish Values		
2. Friends and Relatives		
3. Synagogue Skills		
4. Social		
5. Closeness to Congregation		
6. Great Time		

In the first set of statements, "What I'd Like," you assessed your expectations of a bar/bat mitzvah. In the second set of statements, "What I'm Like," you looked at what was going on right now in the same general areas. Compare column A with column B. Is there a difference of two or more points on any one item? If so, you may expect the bar/bat mitzvah experience to change your life or your family's life in some manner, and there is a strong possibility you will feel shortchanged by the experience. For example, if you entered a "five" in box 5A but a "two" in box 5B, you are in for a disappointment: Your congregation cannot put Judaism into your home. Only you can. Similarly, if you entered a "four" in column 2A and a "one" in column 2B, your reunion with old friends and family may not be as fulfilling as you anticipate. If the numbers in column A matched or nearly matched the numbers in column B, you probably have a realistic expectation of what the bar/bat mitzvah process will — and will not — accomplish.

So, we start — and end — with understanding ourselves. If what we really are like is similar to what we would like, we'll feel good. If what we would like is different from what we really are like, either trouble lies ahead — *or* there is much work to be done. (But don't expect your child, the rabbi or the caterer to do it!)

Although parents cannot expect the bar/bat mitzvah event to positively and permanently alter the course of their lives, there are many things they can — and should — expect from the process and the people who help make it happen. At the same time, those people — the rabbi, cantor, educational director, administrator, teacher, synagogue officers and staff — have a right to expect certain things from parents. Here are some guidelines and some observations:

ESTABLISH EFFECTIVE PARENT-SYNAGOGUE COMMUNICATION

As in any complex effort, the more communication, and the earlier that communication, the better the result will be. How the date of the ceremony is communicated sometimes indicates the effectiveness of communication skills between synagogue and family. You should reasonably expect that, whatever procedure the congregation uses to assign dates, it is timely and fair. If a congregation gives dates to all students entering fifth grade, for example, such dates should be mailed out at the same time. Some congregations give families the opportunity to request dates ahead of this; this is fine if the offer is made to all families at the same time. The congregation should communicate as early as possible its requirements regarding fees, tutoring, room rentals, religious restrictions and other concerns pertaining to bar/bat mitzvah. The earlier parents understand what is required of them, the better they can respond to the congregation's requirements.

Similarly, parents need to notify the appropriate person in the congregation as soon as a problem surfaces: "We can't afford the full bar mitzvah fee." "My child plays soccer on Wednesdays, when religious school meets." "My non-Jewish spouse doesn't want to be embarrassed at the ceremony." Approaching the congregation in a timely way gives the best chance for problem-solving.

Be Aware of Your Congregation's Religious Practices

Synagogue professionals generally meet with parents before bar/bat mitzvah study begins, in order to acquaint them with their institutions' religious practices and with what is involved in the study program. This is important, since congregations' religious observance varies widely. Some permit the family two or three *aliyot* (honors to the Torah); some permit as many as the family wishes; some allow no *aliyot* except to the b'nai mitzvah. Some congregations let non-Jews ascend the pulpit; others do not. Some do not let girls chant parts of the service; some make no distinction between girls' and boys' participation. Some services last three and a half hours; some last an hour. Some require that kosher food be served throughout the bar/bat mitzvah weekend; some leave decisions of *kashrut* to the individual family. Some congregations permit the parents to address their child during the ceremony; others do not. Some congregations limit the child's participation in the service; in other congregations, the sky's the limit. In some congregations, frequent interaction with the rabbi is the norm; in others, it is the exception. The style of Reform worship may seem more formal, with more English translation, and with varying amounts of group prayer known as *davening* which flavors the traditional service so markedly. (Times are changing, however, and most Reform congregations are introducing a more participatory atmosphere in parts of the service.)

Despite the many differences in synagogue practice (even among congregations in the same "movement"), the Sabbath service has a similar structure in all congregations. Within that structure, the young person will be expected to lead certain prayers, blessings and scriptural texts. (See Appendix B for a service outline.)

The Service for Reading of Torah

The highlight of Sabbath worship in all congregations is the removal of the Torah scroll (*sefer Torah*) from the Holy Ark (*aron kodesh*) and reading excerpts from the Pentateuch (Five Books of

Moses) and the Prophets. This is known colloquially as the *Torah Service*. The scroll is removed with great ceremony and, in some congregations, it is carried through the congregation. Already turned to the weekly portion (*parasha*), it is placed upon a desk. The portion is read or chanted, a few verses at a time, by a reader (*ba'al keri'ah* for a male, *ba'alat keri'ah* for a female) or, in many instances, by the bar or bat mitzvah child. The *sefer Torah* (Torah scroll) does not contain vowels or the grammatical/diacritical/musical signs known as trope. Also, as each scroll is handwritten by a scribe, the style of lettering varies greatly and some calligraphy can be very difficult to read. The reader, therefore, is obliged to do quite a bit of preparation in order to read directly from the scroll.

The *Aliyah* Blessings

Before and after each set of verses is chanted, an individual (some congregations permit a group of individuals) stands next to the Torah reader and chants or recites the "Blessings on Being Called to the Torah." These blessings remind us that God chose the Jewish people by giving them the Torah, and the individual (or group) that recites the text is said to "have an *aliyah*" (*aliyah* means "going up" and generally refers to ascending the pulpit to pronounce the Torah blessings). The reader may also have an *aliyah*.

In a traditional (Orthodox or Conservative) congregation, there are generally seven *aliyot* (plural of *aliyah*) to the Torah on a Sabbath morning. In a Reform or Reconstructionist congregation, there may be as few as one (the congregation itself chanting the blessings) or as many as a dozen or more, especially in the case of two children sharing a Sabbath morning ceremony. No matter how many *aliyot* there are, it is the obligation of the honoree to pronounce the Hebrew blessings properly. There are many materials available to anyone who wants to learn to chant these blessings; the proper pronunciation can be mastered literally within half an hour. Nearly all congregations provide a transliterated text on the pulpit, so that reading directly from Hebrew text, while more authentic, is not required. Yet, because Hebrew contains consonants for which there are no exact equivalents in English, it is important that a knowledgeable person review the pronunciation of the blessings with the honoree.

The *Maftir* and *Haftarah*

The last person honored with an *aliyah* is considered special and is designated by the Hebrew term *maftir* which means "concluder." The bar or bat mitzvah is nearly always the designated *maftir* or *maftira* on that morning. It is the privilege of the maftir not only to round out the Torah reading, but to remain on the pulpit to chant another text from the Bible. This text, called the *Haftarah*, is from the long section of the Bible called the Prophets. Following the *Haftarah* and the recitation of other prayers, the Torah is returned to the ark. In some congregations, the young person then recites a speech or essay and/or the rabbi addresses the child. The parents may also speak to their child, and gifts from the congregation may be presented. These formalities are often at the end of the service, but may be modified or eliminated according to the wishes of the congregation, its rabbi and the family of the bar or bat mitzvah.

Know What Is Expected of Your Child

A congregation's expectations are based on its history, its rabbinic and religious orientation, and its flexibility. In some congregations, the bar/bat mitzvah ceremony is incidental to the congregational Sabbath experience. Other congregations do not even have Saturday morning services unless there is a bar/bat mitzvah celebration. Similarly, the bar/bat mitzvah in some settings is required to do little more than chant the *aliyah* blessings and the *Haftarah*. Other congregations regularly hear b'nai mitzvah lead virtually the entire service and the full *parasha* (weekly

Torah portion), as well as the *kiddush* on the Friday evening before the bar or bat mitzvah.

All ceremonies require that the child read Hebrew with some fluency, and that he or she chant and/or recite certain prayers and biblical passages. There is also a hope that an understanding of these texts be imparted to the child in the course of preparation. Most children also have the opportunity of incorporating some of this understanding in an original sermonette or essay.

Congregations generally offer a combination of group and individual instruction to help the child achieve these goals. More and more congregations include parents in the process, and some may require that a parent be present at the child's lessons. At a minimum, the parent should be able to answer "yes" to each of the following questions:

1. Do I understand exactly what my child will do at the ceremony?
2. Does my child have a clear idea of what to prepare for the next lesson?
3. Does my child seem confident and relatively free of anxiety?
4. Is the congregation regularly providing me with a clear understanding of my child's progress?

If you cannot answer "yes" to these questions, request better communication with your synagogue professionals, and especially with your child's tutor. Ask questions of them. They will appreciate your involvement in the process.

Know What Is Expected of You

"Three hundred dollars to rent a room for one hour to serve tea and cake to the congregation when the synagogue feeds them anyway? What a rip-off!"

"Two hundred dollars to use the sanctuary? Are they kidding?"

"Four hundred dollars for tutoring? What am I paying dues for?"

Synagogue expenses are as much a fact of life as a family's expenses. The electric company charges the same rates to a synagogue as it does to any commercial entity. In addition, because rabbis, cantors and teachers devote their lives not to making money, but to making Jews, they should be highly valued and accorded a decent standard of living. Different congregations take different approaches to raising funds. Some charge "dues" geared to members' financial ability. In return, families may use the synagogue building and its professionals for life cycle events. Some congregations charge for admission on the High Holy Days. Some charge a fee for using their facilities and/or personnel for any life cycle event.

But most congregations follow the rules of the marketplace. When demand for a synagogue's services is high, say at the time of a bar/bat mitzvah, a wedding, or during the High Holy Days, a synagogue will levy fees on its members. When demand is low, little (or no) money may be expected: No synagogue has charged as much for adult education that lasts a semester as for a wedding that lasts a few hours.

Know what your synagogue charges for the sanctuary, the reception hall, the kitchen, the synagogue professionals. Get your information early, so you can present your special circumstances to the synagogue administrator, if warranted.

Odds and Ends

Every year or two, I hear about a child who was assigned the wrong portion for a bar/bat mitzvah. After months of work, the child had to learn an entirely new portion in a few weeks. Therefore, you should ask whoever assigns the portion to the bar or bat mitzvah to double check the Torah and *Haftarah* text citation that the child has been assigned. The Jewish calendar is precise, but complex. In addition, Israeli and American Jewish religious calendars are not always the same. If your child needs to prepare to chant a *Haftarah* in Israel on a particular Saturday or if your Israeli grandchild is coming to the United States to make his *zayde* proud by chanting from the Torah in his *shul* (synagogue), be aware that it may not be the same portion that would be chanted in the child's native country on the same date. This is because by tradition in Israel Jews observe one day of *yom tov* (holy day) on Sukkot, Pesach and Shavuot, while outside of Israel the tradition has been to observe two holy days in Orthodox and Conservative, and in some Reform congregations. The Sabbath Torah reading cycle may, therefore, be pushed ahead one week outside Israel, and the Jewish communities within and outside Israel may read different portions for a time. The Jewish calendar synchronizes us within a month or so. (For an authoritative source, consult *The Comprehensive Hebrew Calendar* by Arthur Spier (Jerusalem/New York: Feldheim Publishers, 1986.)

What we want from the bar/bat mitzvah experience is sometimes complex, sometimes contradictory. I firmly believe that it is not the quantity of material that the youngster chants at the ceremony that is important, but the quality of the entire family's experience in getting there. The process, not the "performance," helps determine the degree of the child's desire to continue synagogue and religious school attendance after they are no longer compulsory. The truest test of whether we succeed in making bar/bat mitzvah meaningful is determined by gauging the number of our young people who continue and deepen their synagogue involvement, and who desire one day to provide the same positive experience for their own children.

A Guide for the Perplexed Parent

How to Ask the Right Questions about Preparation

Cantor Helen Leneman

A t the Passover seder, four types of children ask different questions: The simple child, the wise child, the wicked — or rebellious — child and the child who does not know how to ask questions. When it comes to bar and bat mitzvah preparation, four types of *parents* might ask four kinds of questions. The simple one asks, "Why do this at all?" The wise one asks, "Is there a deeper meaning to all of this?" The rebellious one asks other Jews, "What does it mean to *you*?" And those who vaguely know what bar and bat mitzvah preparation means, but do not know everything that is possible and available, may not ask anything at all.

For many parents of b'nai mitzvah, the entire process of their child's Jewish education is a mystery from start to finish. Because they fear showing their ignorance or are intimidated by Jewish matters, parents often refrain from asking synagogue professionals either the right questions — or any questions at all. In this way, they lose the opportunity to become fully informed and involved in the process. While reading through this chapter, try to determine which type of parent *you* are.

Since each congregation has its own requirements for bar or bat mitzvah candidates, there is much latitude in what your child might be taught to become bar or bat mitzvah. It is your responsibility to find out what the tutor will teach — and in what sequence — so you can monitor your child's progress. Common to almost every congregation's requirements are:

- Trope system for chanting *Haftarah* and/or Torah.
- Torah and *Haftarah* blessings.
- Reading (and chanting) Torah and *Haftarah* portions.
- Translating and discussing portions.
- Chanting and understanding prayers.
- Preparing a *drash*, or speech.

LEARNING TO CHANT

Chanting, rather than reading, the Torah and *Haftarah* portions is an ancient Jewish tradition. The Orthodox and Conservative movements have always embraced this tradition, but the Reform movement rejected it for many years. Recently, many Reform congregations have adopted chanting as part of a general revival of more traditional practices.

Webster defines chant as "a repetitive liturgical melody in which as many syllables are assigned to each tone as required." Trope is the name for the system of chanting Torah and *Haftarah*. "Trope" is derived from the Latin *tropus*, meaning "to turn." Jews borrowed the term from the medieval church which used short, formulistic phrases in its Gregorian chants similar to our own liturgical use of trope. The system is based on symbols that represent short melodic fragments.

Trope is a very ancient system, pre-dating written music. After learning the names of these symbols and the tunes they represent, students can apply them to their individual Torah and *Haftarah* portions, singing each word by recognizing the symbol placed above or below it. After their bar/bat mitzvah service, students with trope skills can chant Torah and *Haftarah* portions for their own congregation or for a congregation they may later join. It is a skill that can serve them well throughout their lives.

You might consider learning trope with your child. This could be done either in private tutorials or during your child's study sessions at home. Some congregations, in fact, encourage parents to learn enough trope to chant one part of the Torah reading themselves.

Students need a tutor well versed in the complexities of trope to guide them through each verse of their portion. Because such tutors are not always available, many tutors provide an audiotape on which the student's portion is chanted and which the student memorizes. The tutor then listens for a match between what the student is singing and the tape from which he or she is memorizing. This method is geared more toward performance than skill mastery, but is often the only option when no one trained in trope is available. Parents should encourage the tutor to explain to their child what trope is and to let the student understand that the melodies being chanted have not been chosen at random.

Mastering the trope symbols and matching them with Torah and *Haftarah* portions can offer an enormous sense of accomplishment. Learning such an ancient, uniquely Jewish skill can also enhance students' Jewish identity, and the skill can be mastered even by less musically inclined students.

THE *ALIYAH* BLESSINGS

Children often learn the Torah and *Haftarah* blessings in Hebrew school. The Torah blessings, also called the *aliyah* blessings, will be chanted at the bar or bat mitzvah ceremony by the parents as well as the child. Other family members will also be called up to chant the blessings before and after a section of the Torah is read. It can be a very positive experience for children to teach their parents this blessing (if they don't already know it or if they need a refresher).

UNDERSTANDING THE TORAH AND HAFTARAH PORTIONS

Translating and discussing texts, whether Torah and *Haftarah* portions or *Shabbat* prayers, may be done in tutorials, classes, or in sessions with the rabbi or cantor. If this will not be done either in the school or by the tutor, it is advisable to read and discuss your child's portion in translation with him or her.

Surprisingly, many parents have never thought about asking their child if he or she knows the content of what will be read or chanted. Grasping the religious meaning and the historical and cultural centrality of Torah in our lives as Jews is crucial to understanding the meaning of one's first *aliyah* to the Torah. If the child does not understand the importance and the context of the words being chanted, then the entire ceremony runs the risk of being hollow at the core.

WRITING THE SPEECH

The bar or bat mitzvah child usually gives a brief "Thank you" speech at the ceremony. The rabbi, cantor and/or the parents often assist the child with writing this speech. A *drash* is a longer speech that entails, to some degree, explaining and interpreting the Torah and/or *Haftarah* portion. In many cases, the rabbi works with the student on this speech; less often, the tutor helps. Parents can certainly become involved by studying their child's portion and having family discussions about it to help him or her prepare a speech. Do *not* write your child's speech. It is embarrassing for everyone to hear a child mispronounce sophisticated words or to obviously not know the meaning of what he or she is saying. Let your child discover his or her own meaning in the Torah portion; there will be validity in whatever they find because *they* found it. Do not impose your own interpretations on them, tempting as it may be. You may guide them to a greater understanding, but do not let them write or say what they cannot intellectually grasp. Remember that children at this age are usually not yet developmentally able to think abstractly or metaphorically.

THE IMPORTANCE OF THE TUTOR

Like the rabbi or cantor of your childhood, a bar or bat mitzvah tutor is never forgotten, for better or for worse. Adults usually remember either loving or hating their tutor; virtually no one is neutral. This often propelled them into pursuing further Jewish education and strengthening their Jewish identity — or abandoning both. It is not always teaching methods or strictness or permissiveness that determines the emotional response. More often, a tutor's success or failure with a certain child is purely a matter of chemistry. One adult male in his 30's remembered vehemently hating his bar mitzvah tutorial sessions. I asked if the tutor was too demanding, too severe or too mean. "No," he responded, "he had the world's worst breath!"

Some tutors develop a life-long relationship with former b'nai mitzvah students and their families. I once hosted a former bar mitzvah student at my family's seder while he was a homesick student at Columbia University, and I know of other such cases. A special bond can develop when teacher and student meet week after week over several months. Also, do not assume that a boy needs a male tutor or a girl needs a female. In many cases, the opposite is true. It is a very individual matter which depends on many factors, such as a good personality match and compatible teaching/learning styles.

The bar or bat mitzvah tutor is a vital component of your child's bar/bat mitzvah experience. Because the tutor may be generationally closer to children than any other Jewish educator they come in contact with, he or she can be one of your child's most influential Jewish role models. But even more important is that the experience your child has with the tutor can, more than any Hebrew school classroom experience, determine the tone — positive or negative — of the whole preparation process.

Choosing a Tutor

What choice do you have in determining who this pivotal individual will be? If you are still looking for a congregation, you can inquire about b'nai mitzvah tutors before you join. Before accepting an assigned tutor for your child, you can request the names of families whose children had that tutor and ask them if tutoring was satisfactory. If you already belong to a congregation, you will find that you may have total freedom in choosing a tutor, some choice, or no choice whatsoever. Small congregations may employ only one tutor and discourage or even prohibit families from using outside tutors. Other congregations provide lists of outside tutors for families to choose from. In that case, you can either interview tutors or rely on other families' recommendations. Still other congregations employ several tutors who will be assigned a certain number of b'nai mitzvah students. Remember, if the chemistry doesn't work between your child and the assigned tutor, you can still try to make a change.

You might pay the tutor directly, or the fees might be included in your synagogue dues. Keep in mind that the control you have over the parent/tutor relationship depends significantly on the financial arrangement. If the synagogue controls the payment, the synagogue also controls the tutor. Either way, the fee is generally set and non-negotiable. The rate varies widely by region, ranging from $15 to as high as $75 an hour.

The tutor might be a trained adult educator, a rabbi or cantor, a lay member of the congregation, or a teenager or college student trained by the synagogue. All have their pros and cons in terms of teaching ability, mastery of the material to be taught, and ability to relate to adolescents. Assuming there is an acceptable level of competence in these three areas, I suggest you request a preliminary meeting between you, the tutor and your child. Chemistry between people can only be experienced face-to-face, and it is too important to ignore.

At this meeting, ask yourself, "Do I like this person? Does my child like this person? Is this someone to whom I feel comfortable addressing questions? Or does he or she intimidate me? Is he or she trying to develop rapport with my child?"

If you feel comfortable with the tutor, move on to more technical questions. Many of these may not be appropriate to ask of a tutor employed by your own congregation; you can get the answers from the b'nai mitzvah program director (who might be the principal, rabbi or cantor). But if you are interviewing an outside tutor, certain questions are appropriate and important, especially "Where did you get your training?" The best training for a tutor is from a seminary, such as the Reform movement's Hebrew Union College – Jewish Institute of Religion, the Conservative movement's Jewish Theological Seminary, the Reconstructionist Rabbinical College, or any of the numerous Orthodox seminaries. But tutors with this background are rare (unless your congregation's cantor is also its b'nai mitzvah tutor). Parents with a strong background in prayer skills, Torah, trope and Hebrew may decide to tutor their child themselves, with their congregation's permission.

Your role is to determine what aspects of bar/bat mitzvah preparation are most important to you and your child. For example, if your child loves singing and has a good voice, you will want a tutor who can give your child a musically enriching experience. If language is your child's forte, find a tutor with strong Hebrew skills who will emphasize translation and explanation. If your child is interested in Jewish history, find a tutor with a strong Judaic background who can enrich your child beyond basic b'nai mitzvah skills. If your child is a computer whiz, there are now computer programs for Hebrew, trope and Torah and *Haftarah* portions. Try to find a congregation and/or tutor that uses these resources.

Working with the Tutor

How many total sessions does the tutor anticipate will be needed to properly prepare your child? How long is each session? Will the tutor provide a written schedule or contract to indicate the sequence of lessons and your child's progress?

The average period of preparation with a private tutor is six months. Depending on the amount of material to be covered and the level of your child's skills, this can involve as few as 12 hours or as many as 30, but the average is 20. Sessions might last 30 minutes or one hour. If your child's bar or bat mitzvah service is in September or October, factor in the summer months when lessons may come to a complete standstill and begin sessions more than six months before the service.

Many congregations begin with bar/bat mitzvah orientation well over a year in advance of the event. Most congregations insist on a full year of preparation with a tutor. In my experience, this is too long, and many children experience burnout in this length of time. If a full year is required to master the material, then there is probably too much material.

It is important to know the length of each tutoring session. Some children cannot sit still for an hour-long lesson. They *must* have 30-minute sessions. This is certainly true for children with

Attention Deficit Disorder or similar problems. But half-hour sessions allow little time for bantering or for in-depth exploration of a text, while longer sessions let the tutor interact more on a personal level and ask students about school or events in their lives over the past week. Students will work harder for a tutor who cares about them personally. The 15-minute sessions favored by a minority of tutors are too short to accomplish more than a cursory check of a memorized text or skills. And certainly they do not let any sort of personal relationship develop.

A written schedule helps the whole family be involved in the bar/bat mitzvah preparation process. The child will know what material needs to be mastered each week, and parents will know what to ask the tutor. For example, if the goal in one session is to learn the *Haftarah* blessing, you can ask the tutor how well your child learned it during the lesson and how you can help him or her learn it over the coming week.

A tutor should be readily available for consultation. If the tutor does not contact you, do not assume that everything is proceeding on schedule. It is incumbent on you to keep track of the process and be sure your child is studying enough to stay on target.

If you work *with* the tutor, rather than just seeing him or her as an employee, the entire process will be more successful for all concerned. Remember to communicate openly at all times. If your child has particular difficulties, weaknesses or disabilities, explain them to the tutor *at the very beginning of lessons*. Request progress reports. Ask what next week's assignment is and whether your child had adequately prepared the previous week's assignment. Express appreciation for the tutor's involvement and concern. Warn the tutor if your child has had a particularly demanding week which allowed little time for preparation. And do not always assume that your child is right without checking with the tutor. If your child says the work is too hard and the tutor too demanding, discuss this with the tutor before you overreact and summarily switch to an "easier" tutor. If your child expresses fear or anxiety, ask the tutor to be more gentle instead of merely dismissing him or her. Give the tutor a chance. Do not send your child the message that the tutor can easily be replaced if the material becomes too demanding. Having another tutor will not alter the requirements of your congregation.

Always remember that your child is striving for a personal best, not a "performance" to rival what other children have done. If you and your child's tutor stress this, your child's self-esteem and pride of accomplishment will be enormous. This is one of the most beneficial effects of the entire bar/bat mitzvah process.

THE IMPORTANCE OF BEING INVOLVED

The most essential element in your child's success is *your* care, concern and hands-on, daily involvement. Ask to hear your child read or chant. Show support and delight at his or her progress. Talk to the tutor regularly. Be his or her ally. When the tutor knows that the family cares, he or she will be more upbeat about the whole process. This will provide a positive learning experience for your child. And if you have sought — and received — adequate answers to your questions throughout the process, your child's bar or bat mitzvah ceremony will be a positive, life-changing event for the entire family.

THE PARENTS' RITE OF PASSAGE

Rabbi Susan B. Stone

What can be said to a family which moves into their new home ten days before their youngest child's bat mitzvah?

What can be said to a family which finds room for their whole, very large extended family on the *bimah* during their oldest child's bat mitzvah ceremony? Was it the rabbi's fault that the bat mitzvah girl got lost in the crowd?

And what can be said to the family that refuses to join their daughter on the *bimah* at all?

What can be said to a child too embarrassed — until the day before his bar mitzvah — to tell the rabbi that the reason he's had such difficulty reading the text is that he only has one functioning eye?

What can be said to the divorced gay father whose daughter won't allow him an *aliyah* if he insists on sharing it with his male partner?

And what can be said to the stepmother who insists on bringing her newborn child to her stepson's bar mitzvah services?

What can be said to the child whose Christian grandparents do not attend her bat mitzvah service, unaware of the importance of the ceremony to her and her parents? (Because no one knew how to explain it to them.)

And what can be said to the parents who start crying with delight in the rabbi's study before their son's bar mitzvah service begins when they realize that their child, who suffers from a learning disability, can actually read the blessing over the *tallit* by himself?

To all these people, I quote Zora Neale Hurston, the Harlem Renaissance writer of the 1930s: "Ah! My people."

LET OTHERS HELP YOU MINIMIZE YOUR STRESS

Perhaps you, as a parent, see a piece of yourself or of your family in one of these true scenarios. Perhaps you have advice to offer other parents. After a dozen years of sharing the pulpit with bar/bat mitzvah families, I have learned that such stories are rarely about bar or bat mitzvah. That such incidents happen around that time is not surprising. For Jews, bar/bat mitzvah time is second only to a wedding in the stress it creates in families. What these stories teach us is that while we rightly focus on a 13-year-old child while preparing for this event, the people most often ignored (or assumed to be "together" enough to handle it all) are the child's parents.

Each of the above scenarios reflects the stress of the event and each family's reaction to it. From each response can be constructed the family's past stresses as well as those it will face or create in the future. While rabbis, cantors and educators can only deal, however, with that family's present, you, as parents, hold the key to ultimately alleviating your own stress.

How can you do that? Start by talking to other parents. Peer pressure doesn't end with adolescence. Talk about what is a reasonable party for a 13-year-old child, about how your children act when they are in large groups, about how you don't want children disrupting the services by talking or laughing. Brainstorm about how to avoid such occurrences, and about how to assure that your child's formal Jewish education doesn't end at age 13.

In addition, you must be aware of the psychological, social, financial and personal realities of living with Jewish teenagers. And you must learn how to best use the congregation to help you navigate these waters at this time in your life. Ask your religious school director, rabbi or cantor about child development. If you are unsure about what is normal for a 13-year-old, the school's staff can be a great resource. Use the school's open houses to meet other parents and to ask teachers questions about these issues.

My goal as a rabbi is to make the bar/bat mitzvah experience a less stressful, more joyous experience. But I try to take this one step further: How can I make a positive impact on families so I can work with them in the future? Doing so may keep them affiliated with and participating in congregational life. This will be mutually beneficial: The congregation can become the place where stress is left at the door and the pleasures of accomplishment, togetherness and celebration are readily available.

Rely on Synagogue Professionals

As the rabbi, how do I walk the thin line between being the child's advocate — and looking past that child to her or his parents and *their* needs? Let me offer a simple prescription: Allow the synagogue and its staff to serve you as the caring professionals they are. Recognize that your life is changing and that responses and help from a Jewish perspective are available. Everything revolves around the fact that you, as parents of the bar/bat mitzvah child, are adults. You may need to remind your congregation's professionals to *treat* you as adults, not merely as extensions of your children.

Just as adolescence is a time when children separate from their parents, it is also a time when parents separate from their children. Both of these are healthy and necessary. Around the time of their child's bar/bat mitzvah celebration, the life tasks that adults start confronting center less on child-rearing than on separating from their children and on confronting aging. If professionals in congregations can reach these adults as adults (not as their children's drivers/party planners/excuse givers), they will positively affect families' lives and, more immediately, their children's bar/bat mitzvah experience.

What might *you*, as both parents and adults, do to facilitate this? Most important is to be aware that your child's life passage will affect your family as a whole and you as an individual. From that, all else flows. You can notice the changes, learn from your own experience and that of others. You can then conscientiously — and consciously — craft the course you walk.

Ritual Magic and Family Drama

Finding New Meaning in an Old Story

Dr. Judith Davis

Life cycle rituals are the original form of therapy. Throughout the ages, these symbolic public dramas have evolved to help us make sense of our lives and of the lives to which we are connected. Enacted according to prescribed form and imbued with shared meaning, they work to help us change and simultaneously to remain stable. They help us let go and hold on at the same time.

The bar/bat mitzvah is this kind of drama. Evoking the past and proclaiming the future, it links our progeny with our history and in the process, it makes it safe for all of us to move on. Each family uses its enormous potential, consciously and unconsciously, to different degrees and in different ways.

Depending on how we look at it, the bar/bat mitzvah can be mundane or magical. From a mundane point of view, it is a special birthday event for which the child memorizes and performs a lot of Hebrew words and the parents organize and pay for a very big party to celebrate the memorization. The guests are family and friends who come from all over with gifts and good wishes. Everyone enjoys the chance to see each other and participate in the festivities. When it's over, the guests go home and the family goes back to whatever it was doing before they'd begun preparing for the event.

On the face of it, this is probably an accurate description. But it is not an adequate description. It leaves out the magic which makes the bar/bat mitzvah such a powerful event in the family's life, even — or especially — for those who had not expected it to be. From this point of view, there is something very special, if not sacred going on. Yet, it is hard to describe and, in this age of cynicism, probably even more difficult for most of us to swallow.

This is certainly not something I would have believed before I'd gone through the experience myself and before I began my research as a family therapist studying the experience of families during life cycle rituals. Because of my experience and that study, I now can't help but see the bar/bat mitzvah in this more magical way. So, at the risk of overly romanticizing what most people see as a much more prosaic activity, let me share with you some ways this ritual works its magic, the ways in which it retains some of the mystery of the original tribal ceremonies it echoes.

Embedded in today's bar/bat mitzvah, even in its most contemporary form, are an ancient structure and many ancient symbols, which affect our emotions much as similar life cycle rituals have affected participants throughout history. According to anthropologists, rituals of transition (from child to adult, from single persons to married couple, from student to graduate, etc.) all have three parts:

- The "breach," the separation stage which includes the preparation for change.
- The "transition," the journey, the neither-here-nor-there part which includes the public act that manifests the change.
- The "reintegration," the private consolidation of the change into everyday life.

At the broadest level, the bar/bat mitzvah year incorporates these three stages.

A MAGICAL SPACE

The months of planning and preparation, practice and anticipation, are the first stage of the ritual year. Once we and our child enter it, we are acknowledging that something is different. In a sense, we are enacting a change, a break from a time when we were not a family with a child getting ready to be a teenager, when we were not a family getting ready for a bar/bat mitzvah. As the event gets closer, we and our child become increasingly focused. More and more of our time and energy are devoted to the upcoming event. As "The Bar/Bat Mitzvah Family," we increasingly become known by others, and know ourselves, as special. We are getting ready to go through something out of the ordinary, and it is as if our own changed awareness acts as a kind of protective cloak, an emotional *tallit*.

The bar/bat mitzvah weekend constitutes the second phase. Once the guests begin to arrive on Friday afternoon, the public part of the ritual has begun. The worship service is the centerpiece of the drama. Here, surrounded by holy symbols and caught up in ancient rhythms, engaged in dramatic processions and opening up to emotional speeches, that our child performs the transforming act of blessing the Torah for the first time. And here the community witnesses — and affirms — that deed. In the context of this highly charged atmosphere, we and all who have come to be with us draw closer to one another, experiencing a profound sense of connectedness. It is as if the usual boundaries have momentarily melted. Anthropologists call this an experience of "communitas."

This ceremony is followed by the celebratory feast that further extends and nurtures our feelings of warmth and happiness. Many bar/bat mitzvah families talk about the weekend almost as an out-of-body experience. "I felt like I was floating in air," said one parent. "Time evaporated," said another. "The next thing I knew, boom, it was over," said one bar mitzvah child.

The weeks and months following the bar/bat mitzvah weekend constitute the third phase: Reintegration. Here, we and our child leave the sacred space and return to our more usual day-to-day concerns. We settle back into our former lives, the same as they were before, but at some level, subtly changed. We are the same because, even though the bar/bat mitzvah works magically, it doesn't work magic. In our ordinary lives and our ordinary life issues, we are still dealing with whatever problems, possibilities and responsibilities we had before "the event": Fights about curfew; negotiating custody schedules; worrying about jobs, health, money. The bar/bat mitzvah doesn't make these go away.

And yet, the change, though subtle, is unmistakable. The family returns to its everyday worlds as a family which has accomplished a major task, passed a difficult test, launched into a new phase of life together. The meaning of that change and its repercussions will continue to unfold for years. At some level, the experiences the family has just been through together will have an impact on all that is to come.

That is the sequence on the macro level. If we zoom in on the worship service itself, we can see the three-part drama reiterated on yet another level and in even more symbolic detail.

A Magical Moment

The stage is set. The Torah is in the ark, the prayer books set out, the flower arrangements adding their color and scent to the scene. The ritual performers assemble early, taking their places in the center of the ceremonial space. They are costumed carefully and appropriately for their parts: The bar mitzvah suit with the trousers re-hemmed at the last minute after another growth spurt. The bat mitzvah dress finally agreed on. The outfit for which Mother shopped for months. The new suit Father didn't really want to buy.

Together, the family watches anxiously and excitedly as their guests arrive and prepare for the service to begin. But Uncle Sol isn't there yet! What if he's late for his *aliyah*?

Act I begins as the rabbi, the tribe's ritual leader, welcomes the assembled congregation and begins the first phase of the three-part ceremony. The initial rites and prayers announce the "separation" between the service itself, and everything that has come before it — the normal workday worries and concerns — and the special ritual ceremony about to begin. It is also an implicit announcement of the end of one period in the family's life (the period in which it was a family with a child) and of the beginning of a new era (an era in which it is a family with a child who has somehow passed beyond childhood).

The stage is set visually, kinesthetically and emotionally for the intensity to come. Prayers follow their familiar sequence and ancient melodies wash over the congregation. To the extent that the guests do not understand Hebrew, the prayers hang in the air like mystical mantras calling forth benevolent spirits. The child, whether sitting on the stage or called up to it, looks young, intense, and isolated. That is exactly how "the one who is in transition" is supposed to look.

In the second act, the middle part of the service, the activity and intensity increase on cue. The Torah, the central symbol of the Jewish people, is removed from the holy ark. The child and members of the family are drawn into its powerful aura by the ritual actions they perform: Opening the ark, holding the Torah, uncovering it, raising it for all to see it, reading its words, kissing it, blessing it, passing it from grandparent to parent to child. By now, the congregation has become emotionally aroused, enveloped by an air of expectancy and anticipation. It is precisely at this moment that the child is summoned to the center of the stage and the center of the family to bless the Torah for the first time, reading or chanting from it, chanting the *Haftarah*, delivering a speech explicating the readings and acknowledging the family's role in his or her having arrived at this place in life. It is as if the child has been summoned from the rites of preparation, the seclusion of study, the security of protected childhood to confront this ritual in much the same way as all those who came before faced it. The child is summoned to demonstrate publicly that he or she has come of age and is ready to join the community of elders.

Of the scores of bar/bat mitzvah services I have attended, an unusual ceremony in one particular congregation brought this moment home to me most dramatically. Nathan, the bar mitzvah boy, came up to the *bimah* and stood in front of the large, imposing, gold embroidered ark. Wide-eyed and nervous, he looked heartbreakingly alone. But not for long. One by one, the old men of the congregation, draped head to toe in their huge, ceremonial *tallitot* came up and stood in a circle around him. Then, as if on cue, they lifted their arms towards him and recited a prayer. In that moment, the bar mitzvah boy literally disappeared from view, lost in the folds and fringes of their symbolic embrace. In my mind's eye, it was as if little Nathan had been whisked away to a hidden place where the secrets of the tribe were mysteriously being passed on to him.

But all bar/bat mitzvah ceremonies have their own drama. The child stands alone before the world, his or her unique world, ready to perform. The congregation is silent and intently focused. Will she remember the notes? Will his voice crack? Will she lose her place? You can hear a pin drop as everyone concentrates, willing the child to make it through the ceremony unscathed and with grace. The love, encouragement and goodwill in the air are almost palpable and are visible in every face. When the last note of the *Haftarah* blessings has been breathlessly chanted, the collective sigh of relief is loud and joyous. "Mazel tov! mazel tov!" the witnesses proclaim with smiles and tears. The tears continue as the parents make their speeches, pronouncing their words of love and praise for their child, their words of sadness for those not present, their words of promise for the future yet to be. The performance has now reached its peak.

In the third act, the phase of reintegration, the Torah is returned to the ark, the child and family return to their seats, and the intensity dissipates rapidly. Acknowledging the transition begins immediately as the rabbi pronounces blessings and congratulates the family. The synagogue's president may continue the process with a welcoming-the-new-adult-into-the-community speech and by presenting the congregation's gift to the bar or bat mitzvah child. Whether a wine goblet, a set of Sabbath candlesticks or some other ritual object, the gift is a kind of trophy, a symbol of achievement and of promise.

Closing prayers and announcements about the week's upcoming secular events end the ritual drama and prepare participants for leaving the sacred space. With the smell of kugel and hot coffee beckoning, the celebrants and their witnesses file out of the temple and make their way to the feast. A profound sense of satisfaction and accomplishment prevails.

No, this has not been a tribal ritual in the bush with its physical dangers and primal terrors. But it has been an intensely dramatic moment in the lives of those experiencing it. Its power and magic cannot be denied.

From this perspective of magic, the contemporary bar/bat mitzvah can be seen as a transitional drama with unique risks and unique rewards. The child, risking embarrassment and ridicule, succeeds after working harder than ever before and experiences a flood of approval and love from "everyone in the world." King or queen for the day, he or she will never forget this moment. The parents, taxing their deepest emotional, physical and financial resources, succeed beyond *their* expectations in pulling off an organizational feat that months earlier had seemed impossible. They experience the pleasure of their child's accomplishment — and their own. They have provided the means and the guidance for their child to grow and to shine. In doing so, they have grown themselves.

PLOTS AND SUBPLOTS

When I think about all the bar/bat mitzvah families I have known and studied, what comes to mind is a flood of stories, modern dramas, each unique and powerful. But what strikes me most about these stories is how they are simultaneously the same — and very different.

At the level of the main plot, the stories are all the same and the central character is always the bar/bat mitzvah child. At its core, the event is a drama of the child's coming of age in the Jewish community. Family members are supporting players in this dramatic production. At the level of subplot, however, the supporting characters become the stars, and the stories here are all very different.

In one family, the major characters in the subplot are the divorced parents, and the dramatic tension comes from their struggle to contain their pain and hostility long enough to make their child's coming of age a positive one.

In another family's drama, the child's mother and grandmother become the major players. There, the central issue is one of control. After having helped her single daughter for years to raise this bar mitzvah child, will it be she or her daughter who is in charge of organizing the event? Will it be her sensibilities, or her daughter's, reflected in the luncheon? Will there be gefilte fish or sun dried tomatoes? How will they compromise? How can their combined effort and love be demonstrated?

In a third family, the drama takes on a larger cultural meaning. Alex was born in the Soviet Union. His *bris* had to be held in secret. To his mother, being able to have her son's bar mitzvah in the U.S. felt like a miracle. She would make it as big and as showy

as possible. But what would she make of the rabbi's admonition
that the bar mitzvah celebration be a symbol for the entire immi-
grant community? Would it lead the way towards a life of Jewish
observance? Or would it merely be "a stepping stone into the
world of American consumerism"?

The common theme in all these stories is family and how
preparing for and living through the bar/bat mitzvah event affects
its members up and down the generational ladder.

Symbolically, the bar/bat mitzvah ceremony lets us proclaim that
as a family, we are changing and that the changes are good. At the
same time, it lets us proclaim that as a family, we are stable, connected emotionally (even if, in many cases, no longer legally) to each
other and to those who came before us. What's so interesting is that
it is precisely this stability and these connections that let us change.
To the extent that we feel stable and connected, we can take risks
and move on. The ceremony allows our child to announce, "I am
ready to be treated differently." And it allows us as parents and
elders to announce — however ambivalently — "We are ready to
treat you differently no matter how hard it is to accept the fact that
our baby is growing up and that we will have less and less control."
But even as we and our child shout out (or murmur through tears)
about change while we are caught up in this ritual of continuity, we
are, of course, talking about both things simultaneously. This is precisely what the classic magic of ritual is all about: Being able to pro-
mote change and continuity at the same time. It is a paradox; a
wonderful — and very human — paradox.

TO A RELIGIOUSLY SKEPTICAL JEWISH PARENT

Rabbi Jeffrey K. Salkin

> *"He drew a circle that shut me out*
> *Heretic, rebel, a thing to flout.*
> *But love and I had the wit to win*
> *We drew a circle that drew him in."*
> —Edwin Markham, "Outwitted"

There was once a time when people lived lives of faith occasionally disrupted by moments of unbelief. Today, it is somewhat the opposite. We have moments of unbelief that are sometimes interrupted — *blessedly* interrupted — by moments of faith. Traditional roads to faith seem to be incessantly blocked or hopelessly detoured.

Nowhere in Jewish life do we sense this doubt more than with the ambivalent Jewish parent. Something about the years preceding bar and bat mitzvah bring those doubts and questions to the surface.

Some parents acutely feel the social pressures for their child to "have" a bar or bat mitzvah: "Our neighbors are renting the state of Delaware for the reception, and Michael Jackson is singing, and the Prime Minister of Israel is flying in to do *motzi*."

Some parents start wondering about the meaning of Judaism and Jewish wisdom in their lives and in the lives of their children. I would even go so far as to call it *Torah-phobia*. As one father of three said to me recently about the Joseph story, a tale of sibling rivalry, "How do you make this stuff relevant, anyway?"

Some parents remember their own bar and bat mitzvah experiences with anger or boredom, or a combination of both. There is no end to the conversations that start with, "I went through this when I was a kid, and I swore that I would spare my child this dreariness."

Some parents simply become cynical about the whole enterprise, using something resembling atheism as an instrument of escape. As a parent recently said to me, "I have some real doubts about the Jewish idea of God. I've spent a long time looking at all the terrible things that have been done in the name of religion and the walls that it erects between people. It makes me wonder whether my daughter should learn this stuff and become bat mitzvah. Maybe I'm wrong to lay my stuff on her, but I can't be a hypocrite."

TO STRUGGLE IS TO BE JEWISH

The Jew who sincerely struggles with the life of faith and the life of Torah is in good company. For Judaism is the only religion that has, in the words of writer Dennis Prager, "canonized its critics." Jewish literature is filled with stories about those who struggled with God: Abraham confronted God about Sodom and Gomorrah. Moses, during the incident of the golden calf, demanded that God spare the Jewish people, "or else blot my name out of Your book." Job, after losing all that was precious to him, could only listen for the voice of God that emerges "out of the whirlwind."

Elisha ben Avuya, the heretic of the second century C.E., lost his faith in God when he saw a child die while performing a mitzvah. His rabbinic colleagues called him *acher* (the apostate), and yet he was never read out of our history. More recently, Elie Wiesel emerged from the Holocaust to recreate his life with the mission of forcing humanity to rethink both God and itself.

Few modern writers have come close to Anne Roiphe's achievement in the God-questioning department. In her novel *Lovingkindness*, the character Annie Johnson writes to the rabbi of the Jerusalem *yeshivah* (academy of Jewish learning) that her daughter has joined:

> Your God asked Abraham to sacrifice his only son. Your God is always testing and teasing and placing apples in Gardens where they need not have been. He draws lines that should not be crossed and then punishes when we cross them. His tricks with waters that close over the heads of enemies are as often as not earthquakes and storms that destroy us as well or they come too late or too early. I am not charmed by old stories of rabbis who meet on the streets of Vilna and tell tales of other rabbis who are so wise that they have found all but the last letter of the name of God and can show you multiples of seven that will foretell your future. The last years of our history have revealed that all the wisdom of the Talmud, all the pages of the Zohar, all the oral tradition will only bring us to the ovens with our eyesight already damaged by the fine print and the dim light.

In her own life, Anne Roiphe has reclaimed the tradition she once cavalierly rejected. Many have walked similar paths and raised similar objections: religions, they say, divide people and are responsible for most of the world's evil. The Jewish idea of God, they assert, is intellectually and spiritually bogus. These Jews say they are "areligious," "nonreligious," anything but "religious." Some, certainly, greatly care about the Jewish people. Some, surely, care deeply about something called Jewish culture, though we are increasingly uncertain what that means. But believers in God, believers in the Covenant and in Jewish destiny, they are not.

DO RELIGIONS DIVIDE PEOPLE?

"Why can't people just be people?" ask those who claim that religions divide people. "Why can't there be a universal religion?"

But what would a universal religion exclude? What pearls that are peculiar to a certain tradition would go overlooked or be rejected? Think of the potential theological fender-benders such a religion would have. If you think that the world is made right by believing in Jesus, then it can't be made right by doing Torah. The two mutually exclude each other.

A generic religion is impossible because there is no such thing as a generic human being, and there won't be until the Messianic Age merges us into a great rainbow of humanity. In the interim, we all view life through the lenses of our tribes, be they ethnic, racial, or theological.

F. Forrester Church, a Unitarian minister, has put it this way: We all stand in the cathedral of the world. In the cathedral are a multitude of stained glass windows. We are born in one part of the cathedral, and our parents and our grandparents teach us how to see the light that shines through our window, the window that carries the story of our people. The same light shines through all the windows of the cathedral, but we interpret its story in many different ways. The light is the presence of God. And the ways we see its colors are the ways of our tribe.

There are different responses to life in the cathedral of the world. Relativists say, "All the windows are basically the same, so it doesn't matter where you stand." They may even wander from window to window. The fundamentalists say, "The light shines only through my window." And fanatics break all the windows except theirs. But the fact remains, our view of truth and reality is tempered by the way that our people view the world. The light that comes through our Jewish window is the light of Torah and of mitzvot. It is not the whole light. But it is our refraction of the light, and that is why it is holy.

The Messiah will show each person that the light that they have been viewing is for everyone, and that ultimately there will be one window in the cathedral of the world. Then we will have the same view of reality, one that is holy and complete. But until that day, individual peoples bask in the light that is refracted through their own particular window. Bar and bat mitzvah is the time when we bring our children to our window, point to the light, and teach them that Torah is our stained glass window.

DO RELIGIONS CREATE EVIL?

I once heard a bar mitzvah boy trip over one of the readings in the Reform prayerbook, *Gates of Prayer*: "In a world torn by violence and *prayer*." He meant to say: "In a world torn by violence and *pain*." History has often taught us how effectively prayer can tear the world apart. People have killed for their gods. And people have died for their gods.

This is an age of rampant secularism. It has seen the depletion of meaning. It has seen a new idolatry of the self and of the state. The bodies that have fallen in the service of these idols litter the stage of the twentieth century like actors in a Shakespearean tragedy. More people have died at the hands of demonic anti-religious regimes, Communism and Nazism, than at the hands of all the religious leaders of history combined. The pain of the world cannot be placed only upon the altars of religion. Why not look at the strength that faith can instill, and not the pain or death it can impart?

Simon Wiesenthal, the great Nazi-hunter and a secular Jew, has said that his lack of faith goes back to Dachau. There, in that Kingdom of Darkness, he once saw a man charge people bread to use the *siddur* (prayer book) that he had smuggled into the camp. "If that's religion," Wiesenthal said at the time, "I don't want to be religious."

Upon later hearing that story, someone asked Wiesenthal, "You may be right. It is horrible, unthinkable, for someone to charge another person bread to use a prayer book. But what about the people who freely gave their bread away? What does it say about them, that they would trade *bread* for *prayer*?"

Bar and bat mitzvah are the time when we say to our children: "Listen, there is more than enough to be cynical about in the world. So why not learn about the sources of hope from the people who first brought the idea of hope into the world?"

THE JEWISH IDEA OF GOD?

Finally, some Jews scoff that they "can't believe in the Jewish idea of God." Fine, but which God don't they believe in?

There are many gods that a Jew might *not* believe in: the highly personal God of the Bible and rabbinic literature. The God of Jewish mysticism. The God of Baruch Spinoza, the God Who is inseparable from the laws of nature. The God of Martin Buber, found in an intimate relationship. Or the God of Mordecai Kaplan, Who is the Power that assures individual salvation and personal enhancement.

This swift, cursory journey through Jewish thought reveals something indispensable about Jewish self-understanding — whichever vision of God a Jew rejects, he or she is in good company, since Judaism has never had a strict catechism of belief. The essence of Judaism is not the idea of God. A midrash (Pesikta de Rav Kahana 15) imagines God saying, "Would that they deserted Me and kept My Torah." This is not explicit permission for atheism, because the rest of the verse concludes, "For when they keep My Torah, they would have come back to Me." Let us not be reckless. Jewish theology must not be discarded as alien or irrelevant to the Jewish quest for meaning. But Jewish living is more powerful than being able to articulate a finely-nuanced theology. We and

God find each other in those moments when we, even in the midst of overwhelming doubt, self-consciousness, and cynicism, can begin to live a Jewish life.

Bar and bat mitzvah is a time when we can truly find God — despite it all. Someone once said that there are no atheists in foxholes. I think that there are also no atheists on the *bimah* at a bar or bat mitzvah.

YOU MAY BE MORE RELIGIOUS THAN YOU THINK

The Protestant theologian Karl Barth once said that we should never take unbelief at face value. The surprising truth is that most Jews think that they don't believe. Their actions belie their suspicions.

Beyond Israel Bonds, beyond fundraising, beyond headlines about the Middle East, something about the Jewish return to Israel calls out to us in a deep and profound way. The resurrection of a people from the pits of despair reminds us of God's redeeming presence in the world. It says to us, deeply, that God does not lie. There is a purpose to history. There is hope.

The Jew who gives his or her children a Jewish education, even the parent who does so despite serious reservations and ambivalences, is saying: "I want my child to stand in the light refracted through the Jewish window. I know that my child might wander. I know that my child might become curious about other windows. But I want my child to know where home is, as well."

Consider the words of feminist Letty Cottin Pogrebin. Her children lacked even a minimal Jewish education, and therefore, were not bar or bat mitzvah. Pogrebin regrets that decision mightily:

> I did offer the children the opportunity to go to Hebrew
> school, but my invitation was desultory and lackluster, like
> a casual, "Let's have lunch one of these days" — the right
> thing to say, yet patently insincere. All three [children]

refused my offer, contenting themselves with the vicarious pleasures of their friends' bar or bat mitzvah celebrations....My children *felt* Jewish, but had little sense of being part of a historical constituency....Like many of my anti-religion decisions, I have come to view this as a grievous error of judgement. Because I had a feminist axe to grind, I cheated my children out of a Jewish education and allowed them to reject a rite of tribal inclusion whose significance they were not equipped to evaluate....Now in their twenties, all three of them are casualties of my rebellion. They are paying for my commitment to their pain-free non-religious childhoods with the shallowness of their ethnic foundations.

The poet Adrienne Rich once saw it this way. She speaks of the "invisible luggage of fifty years. It goes around on the airport carousel, and you wait for it, and you wonder if your luggage simply looks like everyone else's."

Our Jewish luggage is different from all others. It has been on the carousel of eternity for the last three thousand years. It is now our job, and the job of our children, to pick it up and to carry it and to make it come alive.

The Family's Perspective

SECTION II

Introduction

We can learn a great deal from the experiences of other people. This section's chapters were written by parents and teens who all experienced the bar/bat mitzvah process. These stories are like a prism. Through it, each reader can see components of the entire picture which comprises the bar/bat mitzvah experience. Each component reflects a particular vision, but their cumulative effect gives the reader a detailed look at the whole picture.

In Chapter 8 by Cantor Helen Leneman, families whose children recently became b'nai mitzvah pass on their insights to parents and children who will face many similar hurdles. Their advice will prepare families for what lies ahead.

Chapters 9 and 10, one by a mother and the other by a father, reflect on what the bar/bat mitzvah experience meant for their families. Missy Cohen Lavintman, education director of B'nai Emet Synagogue in St. Louis Park, Minnesota, writes about dealing with the same issues faced by other families during the bar/bat mitzvah period — and for which her 20 years of teaching in a Jewish school had not prepared her. Neal Gendler, a Minneapolis writer and newspaper reporter, talks about the pride he felt at his son's bar mitzvah service and the increased commitment to Jewish observance that the event brought to his family.

In brief essays in Chapter 11, four teenagers look back upon their bar or bat mitzvah ceremonies. Each essay has the sort of vivid recollection common to memories of life-changing events.

In Chapter 12, which focuses on the bat mitzvah as a *mother's* rite of passage, Nechama Liss-Levinson, a writer and psychologist in Great Neck, New York, talks about purchasing a bat mitzvah dress for her daughter.

Chapter 13 is the account of an interfaith family's experience with their son who chose to become bar mitzvah. Written by the non-Jewish mother, Dr. Donna Hart, it focuses on the challenges she faced helping her parents understand and accept the event. Hart, a writer and educator in Bethesda, Maryland, is the former publisher and editor of *Parent & Child* magazine.

Chapter 14 offers insights for preparing a speech to give your child on the *bimah*. Rabbi Sandy Eisenberg Sasso of Congregation Beth-El Zedeck in Indianapolis, Indiana presents excerpts from her speeches to her children, plus those of other parents.

Tales from the Home Front

Lessons from Family Experiences

Cantor Helen Leneman

My father, who was an artist, was often asked, "How long did it take you to paint that picture?" His answer was always the same: "All my life up to this point." The same can be said for a good Jewish education: It should prepare a Jew for his or her life up to that particular point — and hopefully, for the next particular point, as well.

Good preparation is indispensable for b'nai mitzvah, especially during the year just before the ceremony. Preparation for the child, as well as preparation for the parents. With that in mind, I interviewed several families around the country about that year, how they prepared for it and what they would have done differently. You may want to ask friends and relatives some of the same questions that I posed to these families. Hearing answers to these questions can help allay anxieties about what lies ahead.

Is there anything you wish you had known before beginning bar or bat mitzvah preparation?

One group of respondents felt well prepared in every way. As one parent said, "I can't think of anything that I wish I had known in advance. We had a pretty good sense of the amount of time it would take to prepare for the service and the other events, and we were very pleased with the pace of the preparation throughout the year."

But others seemed to feel they needed more advance preparation. "I would have preferred to have known how long it
might take to learn the readings," said one father. "I wish I'd
known earlier who was responsible for editing our son's talks
and who would have primary responsibility for guiding him
through it. I wish we had all taken more time at the beginning,
together with the professionals who worked with us, to lay out
the whole program."

Parents sometimes feel they are left in the dark about who is
responsible for preparing their child. They need to ask questions of
clergy and educators. A prime example of a parent who should
have been more assertive is the father above who regretted not asking questions from the very beginning of the process. You can also
ask your children what they are working on from week to week,
who is preparing them in a particular area, and how satisfied they
are with their own progress. By not asking questions, you will
remain an ignorant bystander.

"Be prepared for anything" is a theme that runs through the
remarks of all parents who have experienced bar and bat mitzvah
preparation. "It was harder for our son than he expected," said one
mother. "He didn't anticipate the amount of commitment necessary. The Hebrew, which was his weakest point, made it all very
difficult. I wish I could have done more to make it a more positive
experience for him."

Another parent said, "We were lucky to have such supportive
friends and family to guide us through all the uncharted territory of
planning such a big event. Their support gave us the ability to organize and be ready for anything."

Meeting with parents and teens who have been through the
experience is one of the best ways to prepare yourself. If your congregation does not arrange such meetings, arrange them yourself by
simply calling parents of post-b'nai mitzvah students listed in your
congregation's membership directory.

WHAT WAS THE BEST PART OF THE ENTIRE PROCESS?

When answering this, some parents focused on the effects of the experience on their child:

"It was a profound experience for our daughter. She is now very committed to continuing to study Torah."

"The best part was seeing and hearing our son's hard work come to pass. It instilled in him a sense of pride and self-worth, feeling good not just about himself but about being Jewish. Being that age is tough anyway, so having this as a platform to stand on is a wonderful thing. It also showed him that hard work pays off 'big time.'"

"The best part was the training our daughter received. She was comfortable with herself and her portion and exceedingly well prepared."

"Feeling all along the way that our son was growing into a spiritual world was the best part. Also, the fact that by choosing to do this, both our sons chose an identity and a history. Their father is Jewish, I am not."

"Hearing our daughter sing out so strongly during the service, everyone could sense this was more than the recitation of a memorized script. It was a deeper connection: A young woman making contact with a text."

"Our daughter's training and the ceremony itself were a time of personal and academic growth. They helped shape our daughter's identity and move her on a path of continuing self-discovery."

Teens who became bar or bat mitzvah within the last few years responded this way:

"What was important to me was being there with everybody I know and love. Also, knowing they were all there for me!"

"My best time was the 'trial run' [the final rehearsal] because then it all came together for the first time. I felt so secure and so good at that point. I couldn't believe I had accomplished so much."

"I loved the feeling right afterwards: It's done. I also loved being on the *bimah* during the service. I wasn't nervous, and it was the best feeling."

"Seeing all my hard work paying off felt great."

Parents also found *their* role in the process rewarding:

"My direct input into the process was one of the best parts. Organizing the party, assembling a personalized booklet and knowing that, in a sense, my efforts were helping to perpetuate Judaism were all positive experiences."

"Learning together as a family. We listened to the tape of our son's Torah portion, then we heard him recite part of it, then we'd do it, then we heard him again. We all learned his portion together."

Still others found the *social* aspect the most rewarding part of the process:

"We had one of the most memorable family parties that we ever had. We reconnected with lost relatives who came to share the event with us, and we rekindled old friendships. It made us all feel very connected."

For both children and their parents, the positive aspects of the whole experience are a combination of social bonding, closeness of family, and sense of accomplishment.

WHAT WAS THE WORST PART OF THE ENTIRE PROCESS?

For many parents, the hardest part of the process was having to push their children to practice their Torah and *Haftarah* portions and whatever prayers they were required to master:

"The worst part was getting our son to practice! There were times when we wanted to pull our hair out."

"The worst times were when his mother was busy and she'd say to our son, 'Read to your father.' The trouble is that I'm Catholic, so I didn't know what he was saying. All I could say was, 'It sounds good.'"

"Even with all this wonderful spiritual stuff, it was still work. I had to remind my son to do his chanting and I had to check up on him. I sometimes had to take time out of my own work schedule to help."

There is no simple solution to the problem of getting your child to practice for the service. Bar and bat mitzvah preparation requires a major commitment of time. You should support your child's efforts and consistently monitor his or her practice. Taking an interest in your child's study habits — and insisting that study be done regularly — sends the message that this is an important process. And it will encourage your child to take it seriously.

Other parents' negative experience primarily centered on the social aspects of the event:

"People cancelling at the last moment, or not showing up at the reception when we had paid for them, was the worst part."

"Planning the party was the hardest part: The preparations, the invitations, all the arrangements and details. We were adamant that the party be appropriate for the occasion. We wanted to make sure our daughter would feel good about the party, that it would meet her expectations. At the same time, we were concerned it not be too lavish. Making this all work was a challenge that took a considerable amount of planning. It was also quite expensive, even with all our efforts to keep things simple."

No matter how much you plan ahead, the unexpected can always happen. One parent recounted an experience that was humorous, but only in retrospect:

"I am a real planner. I like everything to be ready well ahead of time. So I loaded the car the night before the bar mitzvah service with our personalized service booklets, our son's new tallit, his speeches, all the essentials. In the morning, a caravan of relatives' cars followed us to the temple. Halfway there, I realized we had taken the wrong car! Imagine the confusion of all these out-of-town guests when I made a sudden U-turn, signaled them to wait where they were, and raced back home to get into the car with everything I had so carefully packed the night before!"

When asked if they could suggest any ways to ease the tensions and strains of the event, several parents said:

"A staff! An entourage! A social secretary."

"I wish I'd taken more time to learn Hebrew and learn more about Judaism, which is not my religion."

"I would have liked to have had, for myself and our daughter, more discussion of the interpretation and analysis of the portions she read. The rabbi gave us some material, but it would have been helpful for us to have had additional sources of information so that we could have discussed her portions with her more fully. I looked for sources in the congregation library and did not find what I wanted. I am sure such material is available and it is not too sophisticated for 13-year-olds. This would give them more context and a better understanding of what they are reading."

For children, the worst parts were:

"The anxiety for a few days before the service made it hard to do anything else. I was so nervous about screwing up and being embarrassed in front of my friends. I made a rut in the rug at home from walking in circles!"

"All the years of preparation and the portion I actually read lasted about three minutes. I felt betrayed. Also, I felt a lack of control in some of the preparations, like the invitation list (which I thought my parents controlled). And it was hard to handle stress at school along with everything I had to know for the bar mitzvah ceremony."

Some children will be anxious no matter how well prepared they are. But if they have been well prepared, their anxiety will not affect either the ceremony or their enjoyment of it. Feeling let down, which some teens experience when they realize how briefly they actually chant from the Torah, can be alleviated by the understanding that they have learned more than just that portion for this one day. Over the years, bar and bat mitzvah students should have learned about their religion and culture, along with a sense of their place as adult Jews in the Jewish community and the world.

WHAT (IF ANYTHING) CHANGED IN YOU OR YOUR FAMILY AS A RESULT OF THIS EXPERIENCE?

A frequent response to this question from parents and teens was "an increased sense of being Jewish." For many families, both the process leading up the ceremony and the ceremony itself are identity-builders:

"We now attend synagogue services more frequently. The experience helped crystallize our faith together as a family. It provided us with something to work towards together and was a bonding experience for all of us. We have become more conscious of our religion and somehow feel more 'Jewish.' In some ways, we feel as if we made a 'rite of passage' along with our son."

Other families noticed changes in their children:

"Once past bar mitzvah, both our boys began to fast on Yom Kippur and to drink real wine, not grape juice, at the seder. In other words, they are now among the 'grown-ups.'"

"Our daughter became an adolescent. She was proud of her accomplishment and her new confidence has been refreshing — and challenging — for the whole family."

One family noted the effect on younger siblings:

"They now have something to look forward to: Being in the spotlight. And they have realistic expectations of what's involved."

HOW DO YOU FEEL YOU CHANGED AFTER BECOMING BAR OR BAT MITZVAH?

I posed this question only to teens. Most said they felt a new sense of responsibility and had a heightened awareness of their identity as Jews:

"I became more aware of things I had to do for Judaism, like giving *tzedakah*. Also, I was able to participate in my friends' ceremonies by having an *aliyah* at their bar or bat mitzvah service."

"Though my Dad is not Jewish, I now feel completely Jewish since becoming bar mitzvah."

"Becoming bar mitzvah gave me the responsibility to show up in *shul* when they need a minyan. I feel more of an obligation to go to synagogue. I also feel more responsible about doing chores around the house."

"I feel a stronger bond to my religion, and I feel very proud to be Jewish. We visited the Holocaust Museum a few weeks after my ceremony. It made me very sad to see how people treated the Jews during that time. If I had been alive then, it could have been me. That made me scared and angry. I don't know if I would have felt this before becoming bar mitzvah."

IF YOU WERE TO DO IT ALL AGAIN, WHAT WOULD YOU WANT TO BE DIFFERENT?

This question, too, I only asked the teens. The majority answered, "Nothing." For them, everything about the experience, start to finish, was fine. But some had very specific concerns:

"I wish more of my friends could have come. I should have checked with more of them before setting the date."

"I would have started to study earlier so I could read more of the Torah portion. I wish I had learned trope better so I could do a different part if I wanted to."

"I would have liked to be more organized. I kept losing my folder with my portions, speeches and trope study sheets."

One teen offered the following advice:

"Be aware how much time it's going to take and be sure you block out a certain amount of time regularly to study."

WHAT ADVICE WOULD YOU GIVE PARENTS DURING THE YEAR PRECEDING THEIR CHILD'S BECOMING BAR OR BAT MITZVAH?

I asked this just of parents, most of whom focused on the party:

"Keep it as simple and meaningful as you can. We had our party at the *shul,* used Jewish music and were committed to valuing the ceremony over the party."

"Don't make a big deal of it and don't make it too big: Food, transportation, everything becomes more complicated as you invite more people."

"Make sure the party is for the kids. Some parents make it an affair for their own friends. Focus on the kids and don't overdo the adult entertainment."

"Don't invest too much time or money planning the menu. Thinking back on other bar mitzvah celebrations we'd been to, we realized we never could remember what food they had served. So we decided that food was not the highest priority. People come into the reception on a 'high,' and no one really cares what food is going to be served."

"Try to keep your sense of humor. You can't eliminate the stress, but you can manage it."

"Don't let your child put you in total control of all the decisions because later he'll blame you for it."

"Give your child some choices — within limits. I showed my son my five favorite invitations, and let him pick one out of those. I let him pick the kids' food and even took him to the restaurant for a 'tasting' [a sampling of food offered by many restaurants in advance of a large event]. I gave him a choice of party favors and let him pick two. Then I reminded him: If he was making all these choices, he needed to do his part, too, and be really well prepared. He knew that already because I had given him all that responsibility."

"Plan as far ahead as possible. Be organized. Make lists. Choose professionals [caterers and party planners] who are experienced."

"Keep your patience and a sense of proportion. Take it one day at a time."

"Look to your friends and family for advice and support."

"It's a big commitment of time and money. Don't lose sight of the religious significance of the occasion."

"Don't worry: Whatever choices you make will be the right ones for your family. Your child will rise to the occasion. Whatever party you plan — simple or elaborate — will be a success. It will be more expensive, however, than you think. As the event gets closer in time, you may become pretty frantic taking care of final details: Family arrangements, transportation, party favors, or whatever. But it all gets done. When the weekend of the event comes, relax and enjoy it. It is a special and magical time that comes and goes too quickly."

One of the most interesting findings of this survey was that one person's "best" part was another's "worst." That was evident in the responses of several parents. You should plan accordingly. When listing all the tasks that need to be done — monitoring your child's practice and progress, planning the party, choosing and mailing invitations, tracking RSVP's, buying party favors — decide at the outset who in your family is best at what type of chore and delegate accordingly. Be sure to include your child as much as possible in decisions, whether about menu, guests or other matters. For this to be a family experience, all family members must participate. But for it to be a *positive* experience, each member should do what he or she wants to do and is best suited for. No one should feel "dumped on."

While a certain amount of stress is unavoidable (which is true for *any* family function), it can be minimized with good, open, constructive communication. If improved communication skills result from planning the bar or bat mitzvah event, it will truly be a family's rite of passage, in the best sense of that term. By remaining involved throughout the process, you will send a message to your child that bar or bat mitzvah is the passage to an involved and committed Jewish adulthood. And you will present yourself as the role model for such an adulthood.

REFLECTIONS OF A MOTHER

Missy Cohen Lavintman

As education director at my congregation, I primarily direct the training of b'nai mitzvah in our school, which meets on *Shabbat*. I've been doing this for several years. But not until I had the privilege and pleasure of being the mother of a bar mitzvah did I truly understand the *nachas*, the special pride, that other b'nai mitzvah families felt.

At our congregation, preparing for the bar or bat mitzvah celebration involves the entire family. The process begins with an orientation meeting for parents whose children are in their first year of our three-year b'nai mitzvah program. The education director leads the meeting and the rabbi and cantor each give presentations. This meeting acquaints parents with the bar or bat mitzvah process and with the school's expectations. This also gives parents an early opportunity to connect with the parents of other students who are the same age as their son or daughter. By the end of the three years, these parents will have attended about a dozen b'nai mitzvah ceremonies of the others' children. We also distribute a booklet written by our synagogue staff and parents, "A Guide for Celebration of Bar/Bat Mitzvah," which contains information about various courses available to parents; a description of the projects in which their children will be involved; their children's course of study; a timetable and checklist for meeting with the rabbi and cantor for bar or bat mitzvah preparation; and other details of the celebration, such as preparing a guest list, timing the invitations, and reserving kosher caterers and rooms.

Our congregation offers courses for b'nai mitzvah students, their parents and their siblings. Among the courses for students is the "*Tzedakah* Co-op," an eight-week course during which students do research about charities that interest them, make group decisions about which charities will receive contributions from the group and in what proportion, and then fund their contributions with donations that they make from the gifts they receive for their bar or bat mitzvah. The rabbi offers a course, "Putting the Mitzvah Back in Bar/Bat Mitzvah," to parents whose children will become b'nai mitzvah during the year. Parents and children can attend a four-week mini-course, "*Tallit* and *Tefillin* Club," in which they learn about morning minyan and daily prayer. Younger siblings are encouraged to attend our "*B'resheet*" program on *Shabbat* mornings, where they learn about the weekly Torah portion and prayer.

THE POWER OF PRIDE

In preparing for the bar mitzvah celebration of my son, Norman, I found that *organizational skills* were critical. In some ways, the b'nai mitzvah process is like a construction project and the parents resemble, in this analogy, general contractors. There are obvious similarities: The basic idea or concept, the research, the planning, the detail or finishing work, the time lines and critical paths, the financing. The endless lists that we wrote over the entire process created a need to cross-reference. The best part of the entire process was sitting with my husband in our congregation's sanctuary on the *Shabbat* morning of the bar mitzvah service, first with our son between us, and, later, watching him as he rose to the *bimah* to serve so ably as the congregation's *shaliach tzibur* (community prayer leader). In *The Joys of Yiddish*, Leo Rosten defines the word *kvell* as "to beam-with-immense-pride-and-pleasure, most commonly over an achievement of a child or grandchild; to be so proudly happy 'your buttons can bust'; doting-with-a-grin, conspicuous pride, uncontainable delight. 'At their boy's bar mitzvah, naturally they *kvelled.*'" *That* was us.

Certainly, we have always been proud of our children and of their accomplishments, but not until Norman stood on the *bimah* did the definition of *kvell* became so evident. The emotions swelling inside us as we watched him read his Torah portion and lead the Torah and *Musaf* services were powerful and almost overwhelming.

After the service, we watched our "little boy," who was now a teenager, interact with his friends. It is one thing to respect one's child by virtue of his or her accomplishments, but it is entirely different to observe that same respect emanating from the child's peers. Some of his friends had already become b'nai mitzvah, some were still preparing for theirs, and others were not Jewish. The feelings that they showed — pride or respect or simply a "welcoming into the club" — enhanced our own feelings. As parents, we generally know our children's abilities, and we are pleased when our contemporaries recognize them. When the child's peers do so, however, a certain comfort accompanies the parents' recognition that their child will be "okay."

Preparing for the bar mitzvah celebration made it necessary for us to spend more time together as a family. Constraints of a two working-parent family create obvious time limitations. The urgency of bar mitzvah preparation — the child's need to study, practice or attend meetings with the rabbi or cantor; more regular attendance at Shabbat services and weekday minyans; negotiating with hotels, caterers or entertainers; or simply the need to coordinate with your spouse your respective efforts on various issues — all create the need to spend more family time together, since planning the bar mitzvah celebration was indeed a cooperative effort of our entire family. This included designing and writing the invitation; learning about Israeli trees (which were the centerpieces for our tables); writing speeches;

creating favors for our guests; and writing and rewriting guest lists. Everyone in the family contributed ideas and offered help.

We relearned that planning is a process rather than a phase with a clear beginning and a clear end. Ultimately, we felt great satisfaction as we watched our plans unfold into a reality that was consistent with what we had envisioned and which everyone who attended seemed to enjoy.

TREATING THE "BAR MITZVAH FLU"

Some of this planning had its less desirable aspects. Often, the secular details of the event so inundated us that we could not focus on its spiritual nature. Frequently, we had to balance our vision of the event against the feelings of members of our extended family whose opinions differed from ours. Or we had to help our son balance the time he spent between his public school studies, Talmud Torah, extracurricular activities, bar mitzvah preparations, and the desire to be with his friends. We also had four other children who needed their parents' time and attention. As the bar mitzvah date approached, maintaining this balance became increasingly precarious. Although we were physically with our children, our thoughts were increasingly directed toward the bar mitzvah event.

In order to allay feelings of guilt for not being with the other children as much as we wanted to be, we involved them when appropriate. We wanted them to feel a part of this *simcha*, too. They offered suggestions about the invitation and also learned some prayers to lead in the service. It was clear to me that they not only saw this as their brother's event, but as a springboard to their own. They were excited for him, yet helped us keep it in perspective. They reminded us that even while we were immersed in bar mitzvah planning, regular life went on and everyone needed some attention.

It was especially necessary to keep in contact with our son's public school during this time. The school nurse and his guidance counselor were particularly important contact people. They knew the significance of the event and the school nurse had clearly been through this before. She recognized the symptoms of "bar or bat mitzvah flu" from the headaches and stomachaches she had observed in other Jewish students as their celebrations approached. The guidance counselor was extremely helpful in arranging for relief for our son from some of the pressures of his classes.

LESSONS FOR THE ENTIRE FAMILY

When it was all over, we had learned many lessons:

- Agree with your spouse or partner on all important issues (including *aliyot*, Torah readers, the type and size of the celebration, the guests, the budget, etc.) before getting too many opinions from your child. Negotiating with your child is easier when both parents are united.
- Regularly discuss the importance of this milestone with your child. Encourage him or her to think about its religious significance. It is too easy for parents and children to lose themselves in the secular festivities.
- Emphasize the "mitzvah" part of bar or bat mitzvah by engaging in a mitzvah project as a family.
- Be patient. Your child is an adolescent who may be plagued by raging, often conflicting emotions. Everyone in your household will be celebrating this event. They are all excited and anxious about it. Your children will derive calm from *you*.
- Take time to be with your other children. They understand what is occurring to the best of their ability, but they still need you.
- Attend services regularly with your family so you will all feel comfortable there.

- Read your speeches at home to one another. You may be so wrapped up in the moment that you might not properly appreciate what is being said if the first time you hear it is on the *bimah*. This may be true of you, your spouse, or your child.
- Remind your child that this event marks the entry into adult Jewish life; it is not an exit from Jewish study. Be clear about your expectation that he or she will continue to pursue a Jewish education.
- Enjoy the process. This is a wonderful time in your life and in the life of your child. You will be awash in emotion as it unfolds, and your memories will last a lifetime.

REFLECTIONS OF A FATHER

Neal Gendler

The bar mitzvah celebration of our son Jason was the culmination of decisions I had made 20 years earlier when I decided to leave the margins of Jewish life. I started down a path to intensify my knowledge, participation and enjoyment of my own heritage. One step of learning and living led to another until I found myself standing on the *bimah* before my handsome oldest child, both of us comfortable with what we were about to do and confident in our ability to do it with pride.

This experience, along with my observation of many other b'nai mitzvah services, convinces me that the depth and texture of a family's Jewish life *before* the celebration of a bar or bat mitzvah determines the quality of the *simcha* itself.

Because I go to *shul* (synagogue) every *Shabbat*, and because my family goes with me on the 26 *Shabbatot* a year that my congregation offers programming for children, there were no unwelcome surprises in the bar mitzvah process. We do wish that three years earlier, we'd thought about the effect of summer camp on the bar mitzvah celebration when we chose the *Shabbat* closest to our son's birthday, August 1, as the date of his service. But when a first child is 10 years old, who thinks about his friends being away for half the summer? As a consequence, several friends whom Jason wanted to attend his bar mitzvah service could not be there, although two stayed home from camp for the service. Based on what we learned, we plan to have our second son's bar mitzvah service on the *Shabbat* closest to his birthday in September.

We live in an area where ostentation is not valued. Quite the opposite. Also, we sought to keep the focus of this *simcha* where it belongs: On its religious and life-cycle significance. This was not always easy to do, especially since the presence of a good number of out-of-town relatives would not let events be kept as simple as we wanted.

Our desire was to host a *Kiddush* lunch, a dairy buffet for the congregation that has become customary at our congregation after *Shabbat* services. This also gave us the opportunity to reciprocate for the times others had included us in *Kiddush* lunches, and to do something for *Shabbat chaverim* (acquaintances) we'd have felt awkward about formally inviting to the bar mitzvah service. We weren't close to some of these people outside of the congregation, but we'd have been ashamed to leave them out by having a private lunch.

With more than 300 people in attendance, the lunch was expensive. We also hosted a Friday night dinner at the *shul* for about four dozen out-of-town relatives and an informal Saturday evening party for our son's friends, to which we invited relatives and our closest friends.

SMILES TO MY HEART

All this took much organizing and left us with a bill I expect to still be paying years from now, in spite of financial help from my parents and my wife's. But it was worth every penny because there were so many wonderful experiences:

- Seeing and hearing Jason breeze through *mincha* (the afternoon prayer service) the *Shabbat* before his bar mitzvah service (a requirement for b'nai mitzvah at my congregation). The week before his bar mitzvah service, hearing him skip easily through his first three *aliyot* at Monday and Thursday morning minyan.

We were surrounded by several older men with whom I've davened for 23 years. Their smiles, nods of approval and congratulations may not have meant much to my son, but they went straight into my heart.

- Seeing and hearing my son, tall and slim in his first suit, breeze again through mincha the Friday afternoon before his bar mitzvah service, and then through *P'suke d'Zimra* (a groups of Psalms and prayers, "verses of song," chanted in the early part of the morning service) the next morning and flawlessly through his Torah and *Haftarah* portions, almost tossing them off like an afterthought. Seven years of Jewish day school made davening and Hebrew no big deal: He seemed to take it all in stride. I am proud that he can read and daven better than I ever did — or ever will.

It was, in short, the best single experience of the 18 years my wife and I have been married — a destination on the path we'd been walking toward greater Jewish observance and synagogue attendance.

No words can express my feelings as I — raised in Albert Lea, Minnesota with only 13 Jewish families and having learned to read Torah just two years before my son's bar mitzvah service — concluded my Torah reading and handed Jason's silver *yad* (a gift from one of his day school teachers) to him. He'd already read the first three *aliyot* and, after two readings by family friends and one by me, he was about to start the *maftir* (closing verses of the Torah portion). Jason's Hebrew name is Jacob after my father, who died 22 years earlier and who never knew my wife or his grandchildren. He would have been bursting with pride at our accomplishments — my son's and my own.

The whole experience brought a heightened, loving realization to our family of how much Judaism means to us. We were invested heavily in it before, emotionally and financially, but we are now more determined than ever to keep our younger son in day school, partly so his bar mitzvah service in three years will be easy for him, too, and obviously for the educational benefits.

Growing up in my small city, I was raised without much Jewish ritual or education other than becoming a bar mitzvah and attending High Holy Day services. My wife was raised Reform. Although not yet *shomer Shabbat* (Sabbath observers), we've been increasing our level of observance for years. We continue to work toward full *kashrut* (keeping kosher) and make *Shabbat* dinner Friday night the high point of our week. Since our son's bar mitzvah celebration, we attend services as often as before and have become slightly more observant. Raising children in a predominantly Gentile world requires constant choices about how to make Judaism important without making it feel confining or restrictive.

BAR/BAT MITZVAH COMMUNICATES VALUES TO EVERYONE

Based on our very positive experience, I advise other parents of pre-b'nai mitzvah children to:

- *Attend services.* Your motivation can be as simple as wanting to see what you'll do during a bar mitzvah service or wanting to feel comfortable about being in *shul*. You'll find some lovely people there who will reinforce your Jewish involvement. The more accustomed you are to being there and the more bar/bat mitzvah services you observe, the more the ceremony becomes a wonderful part of a regular *Shabbat* service and not some "Great Big Event." Odd as it may seem, viewing it this way will increase its meaning for you.
- *Don't show off.* If your congregation permits parental speeches, be brief and use the time to help your child set his or her religious compass. In my congregation, we've observed an inverse

relationship between frequency of parental attendance and the length of a parent's speech to the bar or bat mitzvah. Some people have droned on for 20 minutes or more. But those who know and love you already know you have the most precocious child on the planet, and they can recite with you the list of his or her accomplishments since early toilet training. Those who don't know you, don't care and squirm with annoyance at being subjected to every nuance of a child's grades, hobbies, love for pets and victory in the state junior yogurt-throwing olympiad. It also burdens the rabbi and cantor, who must accelerate the service to conclude on time. If they fail, you then infuriate the caterer, whose kugel is turning to leather, which may ruin his reputation with your 500 guests.

- *Focus on the religious significance of the* simcha, *not the party.* You must *show* your child that being Jewish is important. Children read their parents almost perfectly, and will either emulate or reject their values. If you opt for a big, impressive party and not the deep significance of Jewish life, your child will get the message. A bar or bat mitzvah celebration that focuses on its religious meaning will be more impressive than the biggest of parties. By thinking of the values you are communicating to *everyone*, including yourself, you may be surprised to discover how much being Jewish really matters to you.

Post-B'nai Mitzvah Thoughts

Teens Reflect

Norman Lavintman
Maya Jaffe
Jennifer Greenberg
Miriam White

Although the following four essays were written by four teens anywhere from six months to three years after their b'nai mitzvah celebrations, the memories of the event seem equally fresh for all of them. The intensity of the experience and especially, expressing it as a memory of physical sensations is common to all these reminiscences. Such intense physical associations, which are not found in parent recollections, are typical of memories of life-altering events. What the teens' memories do share with their parents' memories of the bar or bat mitzvah day is the crucial importance of *family*, of being surrounded by love and warmth. Here, then, are accounts of a life-changing event as recalled by those whose lives were obviously changed by them.

"Being Wrapped in Holiness"

Norman Lavintman of Golden Valley, Minnesota wrote this six months after his bar mitzvah celebration in a Conservative congregation.

If I had it all to do again, I would change nothing. For me, it was all perfect: The study, the preparation and the service itself.

The first time I officially wore my *tallit*, which was during my bar mitzvah service, it felt like my parents were wrapping me in something holy. It was awesome, in the truest sense of the word. When I put it on, I felt older, somehow bigger than my body, and wiser than my years.

In my bar mitzvah speech, I said that I was proud to be a Jew, and I feel that no matter what I do I will always be different and special *because* I'm a Jew. I realized after becoming a bar mitzvah that I was responsible for following all the laws and commandments of Judaism. To even try to do that, it made sense to me to keep studying so I could learn about these commandments.

I had always known that I would remain in Hebrew school until I graduated from high school. Yet, even if my parents had given me a choice about remaining in Hebrew school, I would have continued my Jewish education. Otherwise, I would not have learned anything more about Judaism than I knew when I became bar mitzvah.

Today when I attend services, six months after my bar mitzvah service, I feel more mature and able to help others by sharing the learning I received. Both the congregation and I expect more of me now, and participating in services means more to me because I am an adult member of the congregation.

"A New Pride in Myself"

Maya Jaffe of Rockville, Maryland, wrote the following essay about a year after her bat mitzvah celebration in a Reform congregation.

Leafing through the photo album from my bat mitzvah celebration, which had occurred only two weeks before, I found a picture of myself reading from the Torah on the *bimah*, wearing my elegant new outfit. Remembering the soft feel of the linen against my arms and legs, I smiled at how special I had felt wearing that outfit. Only 14 days had passed, but I felt as though I had changed drastically, and began thinking back to a week before the service when some of my out-of-town relatives had started to arrive.

**

First to come were my maternal grandparents, followed by my closest relatives. I was extremely excited because most of my family lived on the West Coast and I rarely got to see them all, let alone at one time. This would also be the first time in many years that both of my parents' families had been together since my parents' divorce ten years earlier, and some relatives whom I had not seen since I was very young were coming. But I could not respond to them as if I really "knew" them.

"Hello, Maya! It is so wonderful to see you!" said an elderly woman as she walked into my house. I did not remember ever meeting her, but I had been told that my great-aunt would be arriving. This did not necessarily help me, because I then had eleven living great-aunts.

"Hi!" I responded, attempting to sound as though I was extremely happy to see my great-aunt Ruth and as though I could remember who she was after not seeing her for ten years. "I'm so glad you could make it."

"Oh, we wouldn't miss it for the world! My, you've gotten so big since I last saw you!"

"I should hope so," I thought to myself as I politely laughed.

"The last time I saw you, you were this big," she said cheerfully, motioning with her hand two feet above the ground. "You're in what grade now? Fifth?"

I thought to myself sarcastically, "Yes, I'm in fifth grade, but I'm thirteen. I am really stupid and I flunked two grades." But I politely answered, "No, I'm in seventh grade now," and smiled courteously.

"Oh, I'm sorry, dear," she said, adding "You are so mature, you could be in ninth grade," in an effort to make up for having just insulted me.

This same conversation re-occurred that week with three different sets of people.

All my relatives told me how excited they were that they would be at such an important coming-of-age ceremony in my life. Many asked me how I felt about it. Each time, I replied, "I'm looking forward to it. It will be an experience I'll remember for the rest of my life." I said this without much feeling, assuming that I would not be any different after my bat mitzvah ceremony.

Many people asked me if I was nervous about reading Torah. I replied that I had not thought about it, and that I was not really nervous. But deep down inside, I did worry that I would make a mistake in front of all of my friends and family.

At last, the long-awaited day came. We got to the synagogue early to make sure everything was ready. I looked over my Torah portion and then rushed to meet the first guests. As my friends arrived, the only thing I could think about was my party after the service.

As the service started, I looked out into the sanctuary, a large room with a high ceiling that provided good acoustics. The ark which held the Torah had a splendid curtain with a bright and colorful pattern. The seats were filled with eager faces, old and young, Jewish and non-Jewish, family and friends, all looking at me, smiling at me, eager to hear me read. I looked at my mother, beaming with pride, tears in her eyes. I thought that she was crying as she had cried so many times before at school plays, recitals and just about every performance I had been in.

Finally, it was time to read the Torah. As the blessing before the reading of the Torah was recited, it seemed that the faces in the sanctuary had completely changed. But then, I realized that *I* was the one who had changed by taking part in this rite in which my ancestors (mostly boys) had participated for centuries. Realizing how important it was to be the first girl in either of my parents' families to become a bat mitzvah, I resolved that I would not be the last.

It occurred to me then that my mother was crying for a completely different reason than in the past. She was crying because her daughter was growing up and becoming an adult and a member of the adult Jewish community. With a new pride in myself and a new maturity, I smiled at her before I started to read, trying to tell her that I understood why she was crying and that I loved her. She smiled back at me, and I knew that she understood.

I read my Torah portion with only a few flaws. Surrounded by friends and loved ones, I knew mistakes didn't really matter. I smiled as I finished, knowing I had gained new maturity, insight and a new sense of responsibility.

* * *

I closed the photo album and looked at the cover. The front was a mirror, and as I looked into this mirror, I sensed that I was looking at someone completely different from the girl I had been two weeks before. I realized that I truly would remember my bat mitzvah ceremony for the rest of my life.

"Still Hungry for Knowledge"

Jennifer Greenberg wrote this three years after her bat mitzvah celebration in a Conservative congregation in the Midwest.

As I walked up to the podium to recite the prayers to welcome *Shabbat*, I could feel my heart pounding and feared it would explode through my chest. My palms were sweaty. My head was spinning. Between the August heat and all the people staring at me, I felt like I was swimming in my own sweat. I hoped no one noticed. When I finally started, my nervousness eased. In fact, I felt good!

The results of long, hard, tedious hours of study were being shown off in front of a few hundred people who looked like a few million people to a jittery 13-year-old girl. For five years, I had studied Jewish history and prayers, learned to read Hebrew, and to chant Torah and *Haftarah*. I constantly complained about how horrible it was. But up on the *bimah*, I realized that every minute of study and practice had been worth it. Standing there, reading the stories my ancestors have been reading for thousands of years, I felt important and special. It was exciting to read the ancient language of my people in the sacred Torah.

The best part of it all was sharing this special day with the most wonderful person in the world, my best friend: My Mom who never had a bat mitzvah ceremony. I felt she had missed out on an important part of Jewish life. When I started preparing for my bat mitzvah service, I asked her to share this joyous occasion with me. She said she would be honored, and we spent many hours practicing the service and our Torah portions together. When the big day finally came, I felt so wonderful having my mom next to me on the *bimah* and I was proud at how well she did. Having her there sharing my bat mitzvah ceremony with me made it the most special event in my life. Nothing else will or can ever compare.

When it was all over, I felt sad. It had gone by so quickly. When the doors of the ark closed after I put the Torah back, I felt like I was closing the doors to my childhood. When I turned the pages of the prayer book, it was like turning the page to another chapter of my life. I was no longer a mere child in the Jewish community. Now considered an adult, I was ready to take on the responsibility that comes with that status.

Many teens stop their Jewish learning after they become bar or bat mitzvah. But I didn't want to be like others. I was hungry for more knowledge. There were — and still are — so many questions I have about my religion and what it means to be a Jew and a Jewish woman in the 1990s. On the day of my bat mitzvah service, I vowed never to stop seeking more knowledge and to always keep Jewish traditions alive. To this day, I still read Torah and take classes in Jewish studies. I intend to continue. Becoming bat mitzvah was truly just the beginning.

"HELPED ME DISCOVER MYSELF"

Miriam White of Chevy Chase, Maryland, wrote this about six months after her ceremony in a Reform congregation.

My life drastically changed in 1994. Before that year, I had just been a young girl without a care in the world and somewhat dependent on my baby-sitter, parents and friends. But that year, I left elementary school for middle school and things slowly began to change. One major change was being in an enormous school, with many new people, and new freedom. But it was also the year I became a bat mitzvah. Working toward it was incredibly strenuous, but the outcome made it all worthwhile. Many times while practicing my Torah and *Haftarah* portions, I just wanted to quit. But the importance of this event to my parents kept me going. (I must admit that the thought of all the presents also contributed to my persistence.)

On the day of my bat mitzvah ceremony I was nervous, but friends and family gave me confidence. I had been awake most of the previous night, my stomach was in knots, and I was too nervous to eat breakfast. I put on my lace dress and wandered outside into what seemed like the nicest day of the year.

After what seemed like hours, we finally arrived at the temple. Finally, it was time to chant my Torah portion. As I began, the butterflies in my stomach vanished and I began enjoying every moment. When I finished, I could feel myself smile all over.

The summer after my bat mitzvah ceremony, I auditioned for the musical at my summer camp. I did not have much stage experience, but the memory of my bat mitzvah service gave me the confidence to try out and I thought I might at least get a part in the chorus. The following morning, it was announced that I had received the lead part in the musical!

The night before the play, I was stricken with fear and stayed up late practicing my lines. But the next day, I was ready and excited. The performance was a great success. It was an experience not unlike my bat mitzvah service: I felt very confident, and at the same time, I was having fun.

My bat mitzvah ceremony was the most wonderful day of my life and I would go through all the studying just to experience it again. It helped me discover a part of myself that loves performing for an audience. It helped me grow not only as a Jew, but as a person.

THE BAT MITZVAH DRESS

AN INTERGENERATIONAL STORY

Dr. Nechama Liss-Levinson

I was at home when my mother bought my bat mitzvah dress. It was from Alexanders, a discount department store, whose golden age was the 1960s and whose bargains often seduced my mother into believing that she had filled her needs or ours. I remember the dress exactly. It was long-sleeved, and fell in a perfectly straight line. There was no waist, and practically no bust, offering me little help as my body struggled to develop those features. It had vertical stripes, a white sailor collar, and a ribbon down the front.

I hated it. Even as I write those words, I'm not sure if that's exactly accurate. Rather, the dress, with its classic look and severe lines, just wasn't me. I tried not to think about it. My mother had picked it out. Obviously she thought it was appropriate. My job was to wear it and be grateful, and not to make a big deal of it by creating a scene.

What was really a big deal at the time was that two girl cousins my age, Robin and Jill, were coming up from Florida, flying all the way to New York on my account. One of our first agenda items was to show each other our dresses. Robin unpacked her suitcase and proudly hung up the dress she had brought for my bat mitzvah. It was a twin of my dress. Only her stripes were pink and white.

I hid my anguish in a frenzy of denial. I knew I wanted a different dress. I didn't want to wear the same one Robin was wearing. But the words stayed stuck in a very tight place deep inside.

Thirty years later, we began to prepare for my older daughter Bluma's bat mitzvah. I took the day off from work. We would spend the day together, looking for a dress for her bat mitzvah. Clearly, the memories of my own dress propelled me.

Our initial efforts were unsatisfying. The first few stores didn't have anything that Bluma really liked. We decided to take a break, and went off to lunch together. I took her to a fancy restaurant with peach tablecloths, small vases of spring flowers, and frosted candlelight. Even though we hadn't found a dress, Bluma she was in heaven. "You know," she said, "this is great. Usually, you're in such a rush, you want me to find something right away. This time, I feel like I can go to as many stores as I want to."

I reflected on her words, once again admiring her perspicacity. For the millionth time, I regretted my ever-present rushing around, trying to get so much done in so little time. I agreed with her observation. I actually did feel that, for this dress, we could take as much time as she liked. We would go to as many stores as needed. And I didn't feel rushed at all.

"I NEED A DRESS FOR MY DAUGHTER'S BAT MITZVAH"

At lunch, it was Bluma's idea that we take a break from looking for her dress, and try looking for one for me. I was touched by her thoughtfulness, and together we entered a small women's boutique. Usually, in a specialty shop, I feel awkward. I experience an anxious urgency to please the shop owner by buying something. I become gawky and adolescent all over again. But this time it was different. I felt as though I swept into the store with grandeur, rather than slinking in as though I didn't belong. With a sense of joyful accomplishment, I announced to the owner, "I need a dress for my daughter's bat mitzvah." As I spoke, I proudly put my arm around Bluma, the one whose Jewish coming of age was to be celebrated. I couldn't believe I was the one saying the words, "my daughter's bat mitzvah." My eyes filled with tears.

Although we had been preparing for the bat mitzvah in myriad ways, there was something tangible in making this announcement to this store owner, who didn't know me. Yes, I had arrived at this point in my life. My thoughts sped through the time zones of my mind. I remembered my own bat mitzvah. But I also moved forward, imagining myself returning in a dozen years or so, announcing, "Yes, today I need a dress for my daughter's wedding."

The dress I bought for myself for Bluma's bat mitzvah seemed perfect. It was both elegant and jazzy. I was able to express a part of me that I often kept hidden, something to do with sophistication and luxury.

Mme. Sylvia, the couturier, inquired about Bluma's dress, and sent us off to a store which specialized in "occasion" dresses for teen-aged girls. When we entered the store, it seemed as though we had entered the scene of the Sugarplum Fairy. The walls were hung with layers of white and black, festooned by rainbows of pastel colors.

Bluma tried on just about everything in the store. She chose a dress that was silver, black and white, with pizzazz and flounce. She looked radiant. I felt deep satisfaction that she was so happy with her dress, with her body, with her very self.

A Closet Full of Memories

Three years later, for our daughter Rivka's bat mitzvah, it was time again to look for new dresses. Rivka had been anticipating the day with relish. One of the difficulties of being the second child is having to wait so long and so often. The benefit is that parents have often learned something during all that time. We immediately went to the teen dress boutique, and Rivka chose a beautiful dress in black, with strands of gold and silver thread. She looked stunning, and I think she felt it inside.

As I set out to look for my dress for Rivka's bat mitzvah, I regressed a bit, trying to replicate my mother's bargain shopping, but with the same unsatisfying results. Finally, I realized that I needed help. Again, I took the day off from work, and brought both girls with me, back to Mme. Sylvia. This time, Mme. Sylvia chose a long gown, nothing like what I had initially imagined. I tried it on, and it was breathtaking. We all three said "Yes" at once. It was exactly right.

Why did I love that dress so much, with its long full skirt, a crinoline underneath, satin flowers at the hip? How could this material venture represent such a high point in the emotional life of one dedicated to the spiritual aspects of living? The answer lay in a closet filled with memories.

As a child, I remember once choosing a party dress of red chiffon, when shopping with my mother and two older sisters, only to be laughed at by the three of them. "Are you crazy?" they asked. "That's so ugly." But in my mind, the flounces of chiffon were more beautiful than anything I had ever seen.

Years later, buying a prom dress presented no problem. After all, I already had the dress I had worn as a bridesmaid to my sister's wedding. The apricot gown, although lovely, was picked out by my older sister, and matched those of the other half dozen young women chosen as bridesmaids. I wore it to the prom, but never got the pleasure of choosing my own prom dress.

I wish I had a story to tell of my mother and me happily shopping for my wedding gown. I would like to imagine us at the bridal salons, laughing and looking at one another knowingly. In retrospect, the reality seems rather predictable, perhaps even a bit boring. When my oldest sister was married, my father's dress business made a magnificent gown for her, exactly suited to her dignified simplicity. When my middle sister was married, this special gown was refitted for her. Of course, at the time, I considered it an honor for me to be able to wear this gown, when, a few years later, I too married. The gown was beautiful, but nothing like what I would have chosen. Deep inside me still lived the girl who loved the red chiffon flounce.

BEAUTY COMES FROM BEING WHO YOU REALLY ARE

As I put on my dress for Rivka's bat mitzvah, I laughed at myself. This beautiful dress, crinoline and all, was my gift to myself as a grown woman coming of age. This was my coming out dress. I could be who I was. It was a result of the bat mitzvah dress that wasn't me, the red chiffon I never had, the prom dress that was used, and the wedding gown that was in my sister's image.

I felt I looked beautiful in this dress. But I think that the beauty wasn't really in the dress itself. It had to do with the glow that comes from being who you really are, from being able to finally express your inner self.

As usual, in my relationships with my children, I learn so much by being their mother. Certainly, the real importance of the girls' bat mitzvahs was far removed from choosing a dress. Each of them spent hours involved in Torah study, in addition to a year-long project of charitable activity and a *tzedakah* program. The meaning of becoming obligated as Jewish adults, and of their development into maturity as Jewish women, far overshadowed the mundane activity of shopping for a dress.

What fascinated me, however, was that in the midst of the important priorities of the bat mitzvah celebration, the relatively small task of buying the dress took on a meaning of its own. For the girls, I think there was an increased sense of ownership of their maturing bodies, pleasure in their ability to make individuated choices, and increased pride in their growing selves. For me, there was a gift that my children often give to me, the possibility to heal and grow as they develop.

Journey of One Interfaith Family

Dr. Donna R. Hart

We took twenty years to make the commitment; Josh took fewer than twenty months to prepare for the event.

"I'm a little bit Irish and a little bit Jewish!" These were the words of our son when he was three years old. It was St. Patrick's Day and Joshua was trying to figure out where he fit in the "World of Identities."

Josh's father is a non-practicing Jew. When I fill out forms asking my religion, I check the box for "none." So, when Josh asked what religion we practiced, we said Tom was Jewish and I was "mostly Irish," obviously sidestepping the issue of religious and even cultural definition.

My family is the quintessential melting pot: We are Irish-English-German, mostly blue-collar (coal miners on one side, farmers on the other), hard-working and honest. We were not particularly religious until my parents embraced Seventh-Day Adventism when I was four years old. (Seventh-Day Adventists believe fervently that there will be a second coming or "advent" of Christ and that those who observe the "word of God" will ascend to Heaven when Christ returns. They are strict vegetarians, observe Saturday as their sabbath and forbid smoking, drinking and dancing.)

I am the oldest of five children, none of whom have had any religious inclinations as adults. Of my siblings, I married first, had children first, and am the only one who took the effort to have my name eliminated from the "church books," the baptismal record where it had been registered when I was baptized. This was a final move away from the religion of my parents, since it signified that I no longer considered myself to be a Seventh-Day Adventist.

When I told my parents that Tom and I were engaged, my mother congratulated me weakly, voicing minimal regrets that I was not marrying someone who "believed as we do." My parents had always hoped that I would return to Adventism. They purchased a subscription to an Adventist magazine for us, encouraged us to attend their church when we visited them on weekends, and occasionally made veiled comments about wanting to be sure we were "saved." "Being good" was not good enough; only embracing the tenets of "the church" guaranteed "salvation."

DECIDING ON A CONGREGATION

When Tom was growing up, his family belonged to a Conservative congregation, which was the only congregation in their town. He and his brother both had bar mitzvah ceremonies and were confirmed. As a college student, Tom taught Sunday School for a year. I knew it would be difficult for my parents if Tom and I actively practiced Judaism since that would signify that I had formally rejected my religious upbringing.

In a marriage of twenty years and with two children, the subject of religion had hardly ever arisen. We had eclectic taste in so many things and were both accepting about ideas, people and the ways of the world. Religion had just not been an issue. Although I had attended *seders* with Tom's parents and had been to a few bar mitzvah services, I knew little about the holidays or the cultural and culinary traditions, and absolutely nothing about prayers and Hebrew.

As Josh approached his twelfth birthday and we decided to address religious identity, a friend described how her daughter was asked by fellow students at a college in southern Virginia to explain a Jewish tradition. Though her father was Jewish, she didn't know the answer, and later chastised her parents for not exposing her to more of her father's beliefs and heritage. I didn't want Josh or his younger sister to ever be in this awkward situation.

Perhaps the underlying impetus for seeking "religion" was being confronted by a boy turning into a young man, and wanting to be sure that we had prepared him for the years to come. It was with this in mind that we decided to seek out a congregation where we could learn more about Judaism and where Josh could be prepared for a bar mitzvah ceremony, if we — and he — chose to have one.

The congregation we eventually joined, after researching several in our metropolitan area, was non-affiliated and held Sunday School at the Jewish Community Center. Because this congregation did not have its own building, High Holy Day services were held at a high school auditorium. Families with children approaching bar/bat mitzvah age independently located an appropriate place to hold their service, based upon family needs and preference.

My Parents' Acceptance

Joshua's decision to be a bar mitzvah came almost immediately after we announced to our children that we had decided to affiliate. While time was limited, Josh wanted the ceremony to take place while he was thirteen. He perceived that waiting until he was fourteen would imply that he had been unable to adequately prepare on time. It was obvious he could not learn enough Hebrew to read from the Torah on his thirteenth birthday, only nine months away. Instead, after a few lessons with the cantor/educator who became his tutor, we agreed he could be ready in fifteen months, just after he turned $13^{1}/_{2}$.

When Tom and I decided to join a congregation, I gently mentioned to my parents that we were going to give our children a Jewish education. I emphasized that it was important for the children to know about their heritage, their culture and their history. They seemed taken aback and hurt, but characteristically said nothing more than acknowledging my announcement.

Early in the bar mitzvah planning process, the cantor mentioned that, while it was not uncommon for the bar mitzvah boy's mother to have an *aliyah* in this congregation, I could not fulfill that role because I was not Jewish. Her tone was matter-of-fact, and I was not offended. It was important that she never made me feel less significant or capable because I was not Jewish.

As the bar mitzvah service date got closer, my parents started resisting even coming to the service, let alone participating in it. It was to be held on a Saturday morning, the day on which they always attended church. "I don't know that we need to be part of this," my father said.

I understood how my parents felt rejected, sad, even angry. They feared that their presence and participation would somehow validate my actions in ways that might violate their own beliefs. Plus, they may have believed they might be the only persons present who would be unfamiliar with the whole process.

I told my parents that this was a time to mark Joshua's growing up, a time when he would outwardly establish a connection with his ancestors — and that he would feel rejected if his grandparents did not attend.

I also assured my father, who was a lay leader in his church and had been principal of several Adventist parochial schools, that he would not be offended by the service and by Jewish interpretations of the Bible. And he did seem intrigued that Joshua was learning to read the Bible in Hebrew (most non-Jews are unaware of this practice), that Torah was what Jews called the first five books of the Bible and that Josh would actually be reading from the Torah itself, after which he would present his interpretation of part of the Joseph story in a talk to the congregation.

My parents' real acceptance of Josh's bar mitzvah came the evening before the actual service. Because Adventists do not drive more than absolutely necessary on the sabbath, they stayed with us the night before the bar mitzvah service. After dinner, I encouraged Josh to take a last run through his readings, this time with his grandfather as his one-man audience. They sat together on the sofa with the service book and the pages of Hebrew prayers and verses which Josh had been studying for more than a year and they covered the entire service. For over an hour, Josh read, chanted, sang and briefly explained each portion of the service. Joshua shone — and my father relaxed. Both were remarkably reassured by the proceeding.

"WILL HE BE A JEW?"

My father chose to read several verses from Psalm 100 for his participation in the service. I think he was reassured to discover that Jews embraced more of the Bible than just the Five Books of Moses. For her participation, my mother chose to read a poem which began "Do you know how wonderful you are?" and ended with "Great things are in you, because God is in you. Wonderful you!" It was as sentimental and religious as my sweet mother. My younger sister chose to read the lyrics from Rod Stewart's "Forever Young." She, who had so frequently babysat for Josh from the week he was born, truly meant "...whatever road you choose, I'm right behind you, win or lose."

I was moved by my father-in-law's words to Josh: "We saw this beautiful little baby when he was only a few days old, and at that moment we contemplated many things: Will he grow into a wise, gentle, and happy human being? Will he return in any way the great love we will always hold for him? Will we be around to see the flowering for which we hold so much hope? Will he be a Jew?"

This last question had never been mentioned during the previous 13 years.

"Undoubtedly," he continued, "all those questions have been answered affirmatively. The part about being a Jew has been especially rewarding — not because we are Jews, but because it is a very adult decision that you were able to make for yourself. That alone proves to us that you truly are entering into Jewish adulthood, which is the reason for your bar mitzvah ceremony today."

Because my in-laws had never told us that they consider us good parents, it was especially touching for me when he told Josh that his parents "have provided you with all the love, the guidance, and the instruments of learning that have brought you to this moment."

Most of all, we were all proud of Joshua, who had worked hardest of all of us for this day. He did a beautiful job, a manly job. He stood tall and proud when his father presented him with his own *tallit* and expressed his deep love for him. He appeared poised, though I knew how tense he was. After I read my prepared speech, Josh embraced me. I was never more proud to be his mom.

I don't believe that religious training inoculates us from temptations. But I do believe that self-esteem is strengthened by achievement, by desiring to do one's best. From this comes self-respect. The public proclamation of being a Jew, coupled with the enormous, concentrated effort that Josh put into studying Hebrew and Torah, and the beautiful success that resulted, had just such an effect. The self-respect and esteem grew perceptibly — to us and others — over the months following the service.

In the few years since the bar mitzvah, it is obvious that Josh finds comfort in his "bond with the Jewish people, past, present, and future," as outlined by his paternal grandfather on that special day. By increasing our involvement with the congregation along with Josh, our family has also strengthened that bond. And we continue to do so with the community into which Josh's becoming bar mitzvah first drew us.

WHAT TO SAY TO YOUR CHILD ON THE *BIMAH*

Rabbi Sandy Eisenberg Sasso

Sometimes the preparations behind a child's becoming bar or bat mitzvah do not allow us as parents to pause long enough to think about the meaning of the day. Of course, the occasion is first and foremost about Jewish learning and renewal, about family and celebration. But it is also about that fleeting moment as our sons and daughters stand poised between childhood and adolescence, holding on and letting go. What advice would we like our young people to take on their life's journey? It is not as though we haven't transmitted our values in the preceding years, by what we allow and what we prohibit, by how we live and how we do not. But this is a time for us to piece it all together and wrap a gift of words for them to carry into the future.

At this time of fragile self-esteem, a parental address is an opportunity to reinforce our children's positive self-image, to tell them why we are proud. This doesn't mean chronicling every accomplishment, from learning to walk to becoming the quarterback of the football team. But it is a chance to say what qualities you admire and hope that they will not lose as they grow.

If you can remember that your child is only thirteen, you will know to be brief, not to talk above them or down to them, and not to embarrass them. You want your son or daughter to hear you, not daydream. Neither a reminiscence nor a biography, a parent's talk should be a message.

Ask yourself some questions: What gift do I see in my child that a word of encouragement might enhance? What difficulty do I know that some wisdom might ease? What do I hand to my children when I hand them Torah? What elements of the Torah do I want them to carry in their hearts? What story do I want them to retell to become a part of its unfolding?

Some parents are reluctant to speak. Some say, "What we feel is private." Others say, "We are not good with words." But just as our children like to see us cheering them on at their performances or rooting for their teams, they also need to hear us tell them what we value and what we think. To give a good speech, you don't have to be a writer or an orator. You just have to be a Mom or Dad.

Some parents have told me that deciding what to say to their child was the most difficult thing they had ever done, and the most wonderful. As the b'nai mitzvah tell us, with their eyes and with their embrace: These words make a difference.

Feel free to borrow from the following excerpts from speeches, or let them inspire you to find your own words. A parental talk may be offered during the presentation of a special *tallit*, or just before or after the Torah service.

"UNBROKEN GENERATIONS OF TORAH"

Father to son. By Isaiah Kuperstein, member of Congregation Beth-El Zedeck in Indianapolis, Indiana:

My dearest Daniel, your mother and I have watched you grow up into an admirable young man, a true *mensch* in the full sense of the word.

I have a simple message for you today, a message I hope you will hold close to your heart as you grow and prosper in the long life ahead of you. Today is probably the only time I'll be able to say this.

Today's ceremony is not just a show. Your bar mitzvah ceremony is a serious event in which you are initiated into the greater Jewish family. The ceremony allows you for the first time to enter the Jewish universe as a full-fledged member. You do it by reading from the Torah scroll for the first time. When you hold the Torah, when you kiss it, when you read from it, you are not just using a scrolled parchment which has some words in it. You are actually touching and reading from a scroll that is our Jewish tree of life, our *"etz chaim."* This scroll, containing words copied by hands millions of times during thousands of years using the same exact text is the foundation of our existence as Jews. This scroll embodies our culture, our history, our knowledge and wisdom, even our failings. In it are mystery, mathematics, miracles, songs, laws and even city planning. Above all, Torah is a source of constant, everlasting inspiration for our lives as Jews. Therefore, it truly is like a living tree.

I want you to remember that you come from a family that for countless unbroken generations has held the Torah close to its heart. We have cherished it and tried to live by it. We found wisdom and comfort in it. We were protected and directed by it. During the Holocaust, many members of our family were killed because they clung to it. But through it all, the Torah was passed on from generation to generation. We never dropped it.

It is my wish and your grandfather's wish that you never forsake the Torah. That you live by it, that you find your direction through it, and most importantly, that you pass it on to your children so they may pass it on to theirs.

My dearest wish is that your bar mitzvah ceremony today be the entry gate to a lifelong existence as a Jew who will ensure the future survival of Jews yet to come.

"CONTAGIOUS PASSION, INSPIRING INTENSITY"

Father and mother to son. By Martin and Cindy Lieberman, members of the Center for Early Jewish Education, a non-affiliated Hebrew school in Thousand Oaks, California:

Congratulations, Matthew. After many years of preparation, this day has finally arrived. It took a lot of time and a lot of hard work, but you stuck it out, and we're very proud to see you finally reach this milestone in your life.

You've given us many reasons to be proud. Besides excelling in school and sports, you're a gifted writer and a talented artist. And you have a wonderful sense of humor. You know what you want, and you're not afraid to stand up for what you believe in. Whatever you set your mind to, you go at it with a contagious passion and an inspiring intensity. Even in the face of adversity (and you've seen your share), you never give up.

There is a warm and caring side to you as well. You were only nine when your baby brother Mike lost his first baby tooth. When we went upstairs that night to leave money from the tooth fairy, we discovered that you had beaten us to it, leaving two dollars of your own under Mike's pillow.

Becoming a bar mitzvah is a very symbolic moment in your life, and in ours. In one day, you go from being a child to being a young adult. You're expected to take on more responsibility for your actions, and for making decisions that will affect your life and your future. It's a much tougher world for 13-year-olds today than it was for us. It takes a much wiser, more perceptive person to navigate life's rocky waters. We think you're ready for this new role and we look forward to watching you continue to grow as a person.

Matt, your background is rich and your talents are many. The future holds endless possibilities for you. As you go forward in life, remember that the only people who fail are those who do not try. Continue to accept life's challenges so you may continue to experience the thrill of victory.

"DETERMINED, STRONG, FIERCELY INDEPENDENT"

Father to daughter. By William Liss-Levinson, member of Great Neck Synagogue in Great Neck, New York:

Bluma, I've been giving a whole lot of thought about what exactly it means to become a bat mitzvah. Typically, people will tell you that now you are a full-fledged, responsible Jew. But I've always found that there is some profound psychological insight or meaning in Jewish life-cycle rituals, and here it doesn't seem to fit. At age twelve, when you're on the cusp of adolescence, seeking to be independent, struggling to define who you are, rebelling against excessive controls and responsibilities that aren't of your choosing, we say, "Poof, you are responsible and liable for all the commandments"? I think not. The very fact that the Hebrew term for your coming-of-age is bat mitzvah — daughter of commandment — and not "*baalat mitzvah*," which would be the Hebrew way of saying that you are truly master of the commandments, one who owns them and is held liable, tells me something very different. As you have grown from infancy to a toddler, a young child to a pre-adolescent, one thing remains constant: You are and always will be our daughter. And as our daughter, there is a bond that connects us to you, and makes all of us responsible to work, to love, to give and take as a family.

We don't always have the answers, and we don't always succeed. But that bond tells us that we must assume the responsibility of struggling to find ourselves as individuals and as a family unit. So, too, you as a bat mitzvah are not expected now to miraculously have total mastery of Judaism, for we *each* remain bar or bat mitzvah, a son or daughter, forever responsible to participate in the process, in the struggle.

Being a Jew is very much a personal process. No one but you yourself can define what your relationship to God is, and you must find your own meaning in Judaism, our history, culture, laws and practices, for it to be meaningful to you. As Moses said, "This is my God and I will glorify him." Yet, Moses also knew that "This is the God of my ancestors."

In your brief twelve years, you have learned a great deal, from Mommy and me, and from your teachers in your school, about Jewish religion and history. This is a framework for you, one to which you also bring wonderful qualities of your own, for you are determined, strong, fiercely independent.

I love you very much and am very proud of you. I hope that Mommy and I can always help you and guide you, whenever you need and want that. But most of all, we will be there to give you our love and support as you continue to grow and become a Jewish woman.

"SILLINESS AND TEARS"

Mother to daughter. By Rabbi Sandy Eisenberg Sasso and her husband Rabbi Dennis Sasso, of Congregation Beth-El Zedeck in Indianapolis:

It seems like only yesterday that we stood with you on this *bimah* to welcome you into the covenant of the Jewish people and give you your Hebrew name. We were afraid then that you would cry. Now, I am afraid that I will.

What do I wish for you, my little girl becoming a woman, my daughter with the enchanted smile:

> I wish for you to be a
> person of character
> strong but not tough,
> gentle but not weak.
>
> I wish for you to be
> righteous but not self-righteous
> honest but not unforgiving.
>
> Wherever you journey, may your steps be firm
> and may you walk in just paths
> and not be afraid.
> Whenever you speak, may your words
> be words of wisdom and friendship.

May your hands build
and your heart preserve what is good
and beautiful in our world.

May the voices of the generations of our people
move through you
and may the God of our ancestors
be your God as well.

May you know that there is a people,
a rich heritage, to which you belong
and from that sacred place
you are connected to all who dwell on the earth.

May the stories of our people
be upon your heart
and the grace of the Torah rhythm
dance in your soul.

My daughter, we'd like to clear every path for you, pick up the stones over which you may stumble, light all the dark places. We know we cannot. There are journeys you will undertake on your own. We'd like to think we have given you the common sense, the inner courage and the humor to maneuver your way among the stones and light the night. We want you to know that it's okay to stumble. There is no prima ballerina who has never fallen. Grace is in knowing how to stand up again and keep dancing.

There was a time when women were told what they could *not* be. Then there came a time when women were told what they *needed* to be, if they wanted success. I want you to know: There is nothing as a woman that you cannot be. And there are only two things you need to be: true to yourself, and responsible to your community.

Sometimes, the most beautiful things you can create are acts of lovingkindness. You have the uncanny ability to know when someone is hurt and the graciousness to make it better with the touch of your hand. It is a great gift. Don't compare yourself to others. Be yourself. Know your own greatness.

As you continue to grow, we will tell you to be somewhat cautious, and we'll encourage you to doubt, to question and challenge, to look beneath the surface. But we also want you to trust yourself and trust life's possibilities. We want you to believe in goodness, in dreams, to have faith. Don't take foolish risks, but do not be afraid to take a chance on something important even if it seems improbable. You may just discover the wings that will allow you to soar. For all your changes, keep your wonder, your spirit and your smile.

We share so much. We laugh at each other's silliness and shed tears at the same movies. We can speak to each other without words. I watch you with great pride. As hard as it is to let go of my little girl, it is wonderful to hold the hand of my growing up daughter.

When I was little, I used to keep a diary. You and I read through it recently, and we couldn't stop laughing. At the end of each entry, I would write "This has been a wonderful day." It was my own tradition. In that ancient tradition, I say to you, "This has been a really wonderful day." We love you very much.

"ALWAYS HAVE HEROES AND HEROINES"

Mother to son. By Rabbi Sandy Eisenberg Sasso:
Today is a mark of your becoming a man. Some people say being a man means being tough. Being tough when you should be kind is the mark of a fool, not the measure of a man. We measure a man not by his height or the size of his muscles, but by the breadth of his wisdom and the expanse of his heart.

There are many things that Dad and I want you to know as you grow into Jewish manhood. We want you to have a sense of history;

to know about those people whose discoveries expanded our knowledge. Read about those people who worked for peace, equality, healing, justice, beauty. Understand what it must have meant for those men and women to have taken risks, to have dared. Appreciate the contribution of those who composed the music and wrote the words that still move us to great heights and touch our deepest soul. I've seen you marvel at a composer's inspiration and skill and at a scientist's inventiveness and knowledge. I hope you'll always have heroes and heroines to whose values you can aspire.

We also would like you to know about those people whose names we do not know. Think about men and women who never wrote a word, but who helped heal the sick, who welcomed the stranger, who taught the children, who planted the trees in whose shade we now sit. They are all your ancestors. They gave you a past; you can give them a future.

One of the things we would like you to know as you become a bar mitzvah is about God — from life, not from a textbook. We'd like you to see God in acts of kindness, in a great music composition, in nature, in the search for knowledge, the pursuit of peace. We would like you to find God in yourself and in others, in the heavens and somewhere in your bedroom with its pile of clothes and sheets of music and books. We'd like you to find God somewhere between the black and white keys on your piano, in the order of a mathematical equation and in the breath that makes music from the reed of your saxophone. We'd like you to bring God into the everyday by being a friend, by being sad when people hurt and destroy. We'd like you to bring God into the world by throwing litter in garbage cans, by putting coins in your *tzedakah* box, by making music, by a sense of humor, of gratitude, of joy.

We wish you the wisdom to know that our Jewish principles of justice and fairness really do have something to do with the lives we lead. We don't just want you to "do well," but also to act well, be fair, decent, honorable and considerate. When we see you doing that, as you have in your own quiet way, we're filled with pride.

Just as we still need to remind you to clean up your room and not to throw your coat on the kitchen table or leave gum wrappers in your pants pockets, you'll probably have to remind us that the little boy we rocked in our arms and carried on our shoulders and walked the floors with until 3:00 a.m. is growing up. As you go and grow into this exciting new time in your life, we'll try and let go a little, but we'll always be there when you need us. Remember that no matter how grown up you are, we'll always be your Mom and Dad, and you'll always be our son whom we love.

Essentials and Options for the Service and the Celebration

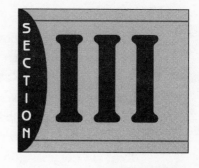

Introduction

The main road for a traditional bar/bat mitzvah ceremony has markers that are well-proven and time-tested: Those seeking tradition can largely follow what has preceded them, which has surely worked for preceding generations of bar/bat mitzvah teens and their parents. This section focuses on detours from this main road: Issues and hurdles that arise when contemplating creating an innovative service; or when ex-spouses negotiate about the service or the celebration; or when interfaith families try to navigate their way through the potential theological and emotional thickets of the bar/bat mitzvah of their child.

Chapter 15 by Cantor Helen Leneman focuses on how to create a personalized service booklet, and suggests readings to include in such a booklet. Options for unaffiliated families who wish to create their own bar/bat mitzvah service are also discussed.

In Chapter 16, Sally Weber, L.C.S.W. discusses how divorced families can negotiate in advance of a bar or bat mitzvah celebration to avoid unnecessary and unpleasant conflicts. Weber, regional director of Jewish Family Services of Los Angeles for the San Fernando Valley, explains how all concerned can work together to create harmony rather than dissonance.

In Chapter 17, Rabbi Aaron Bergman of Congregation Beth Abraham Hillel Moses in West Bloomfield, Michigan, discusses "themes" in today's bar and bat mitzvah celebrations and how their popularity reflects parents' great love and care for their children. He suggests how the theme can be woven more tightly into the fabric of Jewish tradition.

Chapter 18, also by Cantor Leneman, gives a brief overview of the function of a party planner. It will help you decide whether or not to use such services.

Chapters 19 and 20 both discuss the internal dynamics of interfaith families at bar/bat mitzvah time and how such families might decide to raise their child as a Jew. The authors bring many years of experience to these chapters. Joan Hawxhurst, who wrote Chapter 19, founded *Dovetail,* the only independent national periodical devoted exclusively to the challenges and opportunities of life in an interfaith family. She discusses a variety of possible approaches for interfaith families to use this important rite of passage as a means of enrichment for their family and of affirming identity for their child.

Lena Romanoff, who wrote Chapter 20, founded and directs the Jewish Converts & Interfaith Network, an organization for Jews by Choice and for those involved in an interfaith relationship. Using advice gleaned from counseling thousands of families, Romanoff suggests strategies for including the non-Jewish parent and other relatives in bar/bat mitzvah preparation and in the ceremony itself.

In Chapter 21, Beverly Weaver, a tutor of special needs children in Alexandria, Virginia, and Washington, D.C., recounts the two-year process of preparing her own son, who had special learning needs, for his bar mitzvah ceremony.

DESIGNING A CREATIVE SERVICE

Cantor Helen Leneman

Designing a creative bar/bat mitzvah service personalizes the event and gives family members new opportunities to participate in the service. Congregations vary in the amount of latitude they give families to design their children's services, with Reform and Reconstructionist congregations usually allowing the greatest amount of freedom and creativity. The appeal of creating a service may be the sense of control and empowerment. When having a creative service, many congregations encourage creating a personalized booklet or at least, a small collection of readings culled from many sources. Some provide a great deal of participation by family members during the service, while others provide none or very little.

You should discuss these issues with the professionals in your congregation well in advance of your child's bar or bat mitzvah service. Be clear about your needs and desires, but recognize that you will be expected to adhere to the standards of your congregation.

GUIDELINES FOR THE UNAFFILIATED

Sixty-three percent of American Jews are not affiliated with a congregation. If you do not wish to join a congregation, yet want your child to have a bar or bat mitzvah service, you have several options:

- You can locate a group, where you and your family can find a sense of community and where your child can celebrate a bar or bat mitzvah service. These include *havurot*, participant-led groups that meet regularly for *Shabbatot* and holiday services.
- You can find a person capable of teaching your child the skills necessary for a meaningful bar or bat mitzvah service. This person, who might also lead your service, should be an experienced Jewish educator, but does not necessarily have to be a rabbi or a cantor, since neither is required to conduct a bar/bat mitzvah service. But to gain a sense of community, it is best for your child to study alongside other children. For this, you might find a Jewish educator who independently teaches small groups of children, or a Sunday School that is not affiliated with a congregation.

Once you have found a group or a person, you may still need to find a location for the service itself. Some congregations rent their main sanctuary or a small chapel on those days when they are not being used by the congregation. Another option is to rent a chapel at a local Hillel connected to a university, or your local Jewish Community Center might have a chapel for rent.

Some sites might be more readily available on a Saturday evening, when you can conduct a *Shabbat* late afternoon/early evening service (*Mincha/Maariv*) that concludes with the *Havdalah* ceremony, which includes such lovely rituals as lighting a braided candle and smelling sweet spices, can be done by candlelight and often includes such popular melodies as *Eliayahu Hanavi*. If you have access to a Torah and a portable ark, you might rent a non-religious site such as a hotel reception room or a country club, or you can even use your living room or backyard. Any space with a Torah and an ark becomes a holy space when used for *Shabbat* services.

As a first step, contact your local Jewish Community Center or your Board of Jewish Education for a list of names of small *havurot*; or of educators who prepare children in bar/bat mitzvah skills and might even be able to lead your service (or at least who will know someone who can); or of Sunday Schools not affiliated with congregations.

THE SERVICE BOOKLET

For creative services, personalized service booklets have become popular in recent years. These booklets supplement the regular *siddur* (prayer book) and include readings and sometimes prayers. But the kind of booklet discussed here would *replace* the prayer book and be produced primarily by families who do not belong to a congregation.

Three elements go into a service booklet:

- The essential prayers, in Hebrew as well as optional English translations and/or transliterations.
- Appropriate selections in English, either for silent meditation or responsive readings.
- Artwork, such as clip art or original drawings.

Design and layout of these booklets are your responsibility, but it is preferable to have an experienced Jewish professional guide you to ensure that the booklet includes the essential elements of a service. Congregations often provide members with booklets produced by previous families as a guideline.

The best sources for readings (besides other people's booklets) are prayer books published by the Reform, Reconstructionist and Conservative movements. (See Appendix D for a bibliography of these prayer books.) These can be found in synagogue libraries or in the library of a Jewish Community Center or a local Board of Jewish Education. You may be able to borrow them from your rabbi or cantor. Though any non-Orthodox synagogue service usually includes some English readings, a personalized booklet lets you choose readings that are particularly meaningful to you and your family.

Select readings that speak to your family personally, and choose several readings that will work as responsive readings. You may ask family or friends to lead the congregation in these readings.

Since most congregations that let families create their own booklets are Reform, here is an outline of the core elements of a Reform *Shabbat* service. Most of these same elements are in Conservative and Reconstructionist services.

> *Welcome; Shabbat Shalom*
> *Barchu*
> *Sh'ma/V'Ahavta*
> *Mi Chamocha*
> *Amidah*
> *Silent Meditation*
> *Oseh Shalom*
> *Torah Service*
> *Aleinu*
> *Mourner's Kaddish*
> *Adon Olam or Eyn Keloheinu*

CREATE CATEGORIES

When collecting readings, it is good to think in terms of the categories of the worship service. One category that could include a reading might be "*Shabbat*" or "*prayer*." You might even include several readings dealing with these topics. Appendix D provides a list of books containing readings which can be used in your personalized service booklet.

The next category might be the "*Sh'ma*" and "*V'Ahavta*" section. Many modern poems reinterpret these prayers for a modern sensibility. For example, "*Sh'ma*" means "Hear" and is the opening word of "Hear O Israel, the Lord our God, the Lord is One." Modern readings talk of the difference between "to hear" and "to listen." "*V'Ahavta*" means "And you shall love [the Lord your God]." A modern interpretation of this might focus on the meaning of being commanded to love, or ways in which this love can manifest itself.

The "*amidah*" prayer includes the "*kedushah*," or "sanctification." Modern poems and readings address the different meanings that "holiness" can have for us today or how we can find holiness in our lives.

During or after the *amidah*, there is usually a period of silent meditation. This part of the booklet can include a variety of inspirational quotes from varied thinkers, writer and poets. Albert Einstein, Maimonides, Lawrence Kushner, Elie Wiesel, Leah Goldberg and Anne Frank have been included in booklets.

Generations of Jews have dreamed of peace. To coincide with the singing of "*Oseh Shalom*," "*Sim Shalom*," or "*Shalom Rav*," any of which might follow the *amidah*, poems about peace could be included in the booklet. The Israeli poet Yehuda Amichai's poems on peace have been beautifully translated, as have other modern poets. Quotes from the prophets on the same topic are also appropriate.

The Torah has inspired wonderful modern poems, any of which can enhance the Torah Service section of the booklet. As with all the other readings, the purpose is to make the prayers more relevant. Putting a fresh face on readings that have been taken for granted and done by rote for too long makes the service more interesting and special.

If the personalized service booklet is the only book being used during your service, remember to include in it copies of your child's Torah and *Haftarah* portions, in Hebrew and in English, for the congregation to follow. Of course, a *chumash* (a book containing the Five Books of Moses in Hebrew and English) is preferable as it lends context to the reading. If a *chumash* cannot be made available to everyone attending the service, the bar or bat mitzvah child or the service leader may simply explain how the reading fits into the yearly cycle.

At the conclusion of the Torah service, parents usually say a few personal words of congratulations to their child. Some parents are comfortable writing and speaking their own words. But for those who are not, there are many wonderful and appropriate poems that can be read. One that has become popular is an adaptation of the Rudyard Kipling poem, "If," in which the child's own name is inserted in the last line. This poem opens with the lines:

> *If you can keep your head when all about you*
> *Are losing theirs and blaming it on you...*

and ends with:

> *Yours is the Earth and everything that's in it,*
> *And, which is more, my (son's/daughter's name),*
> *you can reach for the sun.*

There are also inspiring poems about children that can be included in this part of the booklet. One particularly moving poem is "We Pray for Children" by Ina Hughes.

The *Mourner's Kaddish* is always said near the conclusion of the *Shabbat* service. Poems about death are appropriate at this point of the service, and may be read aloud or silently. These often provide an opportunity to remember cherished family members who could not share the joy of this special day. Both bar/bat mitzvah and death are key life cycle events, and poems linking the two can be included in the booklet.

As for artwork in your booklet, it is advisable to purchase Jewish clip art, which is now available in many Jewish book stores. The cost of a computer disk with art can be as low as $35. One excellent source for Judaic software is Davka Corporation (tel. 800-621-8227). Some Jewish clip art can also be found through desktop publishing companies. An artistic family member, of course, can design a very personalized booklet which could include original drawings. Although many families create successful booklets by cutting and pasting material photocopied from other booklets, be aware of copyright laws.

Assembling and designing a personalized service booklet for your child's bar or bat mitzvah ceremony is a challenging and, ultimately, very rewarding job. All your hard work will produce a very meaningful memento that can be handed down from generation to generation within your family. The bar/bat mitzvah ceremony often goes by so quickly that most families experience it in a sort of daze, but the booklet will remain as a physical reminder of one of the most precious days in a Jewish family's life.

CELEBRATING AND NEGOTIATING

AVOIDING A POST-DIVORCE BATTLE ON THE *BIMAH*

Sally Weber

You have waited for this day for 13 years. In your head — and your heart — you have anticipated the pride, the love and the excitement you would feel as your first child becomes bar/bat mitzvah. The service will be held at the congregation where you have been a member for years. Friends, family, *havurah* members, community — all will attend and share this special day with you.

But there is something you had not anticipated, something not part of the plans or the fantasies. On this day, you and your former spouse will share pride in your child's *simcha*, but you will not share it together. He or she will sit on one side of the aisle, you on the other. In fact, this occasion may mark not only your child's bar or bat mitzvah, but possibly the first major "public appearance" of your family since your divorce.

YOU DIVORCED EACH OTHER, NOT YOUR CHILD

How you and your family experience this day, and how your child remembers it, depends on many factors. Some are private, bound up in the relationships of the family. But some depend on how you, as a family, are guided and supported by your congregation. The most important thing to remember is that the bar/bat mitzvah ceremony honors the family in general, but your child in particular. Families get into trouble when "left over" issues from a failed marriage overtake the focus of the bar/bat mitzvah. In the best and most amicable of divorces, there will be emotional baggage, but one thing is almost universally true: Neither of you divorced your child. Because of this, there is room to negotiate how you, as parents, can bring this event off with pride, celebration and love.

The second important thing to remember is that all bar/bat mitzvah celebrations are stressful, and not merely because of the pressure on the child to study, learn and "perform." They are also stressful because of the change going on in the family: All those issues of "letting go" which have been building up since your child took his or her first step. These are suddenly being brought into focus. This *simcha* not only celebrates growth and change for the child; it similarly denotes a major transition for the family.

Along with the pride and pleasure one feels watching a child approach this extraordinary benchmark is the twinge one feels that adolescence is just beginning, that the family is approaching yet another time of change. While change is exciting, challenging and often creative, it is also stressful.

Much of parents' worries and frantic activity around the bar/bat mitzvah event is displaced anxiety: How will out-of-town family members or friends judge you? What kind of impression do you want to make? The parents' real focus should be their child, not themselves, but anxieties often mount and escalate in direct proportion to the emotional vestiges of a divorce.

In a divorced family, issues connected to decision-making (How many people can we invite? What should the invitations say? Who will present the *tallit*?) can be especially difficult. The mechanisms for negotiation have often broken down, and each decision is laden with a multitude of unresolved issues from the marriage. And because of the changes brought about through remarriage, the families are often much more complicated.

Many divorced and remarried families approach a bar/bat mitzvah event with a sense of crisis. All the issues of the marriage, birth of the children, hopes, dreams and expectations, and ultimate coming apart of the family unit converge at once. In addition, divorced and remarried families often feel invisible to the Jewish community. This can be particularly true with a remarried family: If the child's name and the family name remain the same, one can go for a long time in a congregation without the nature of the family system being known or understood. Rabbis, cantors and educators are not always aware of the existence of parents and family members who are not active in their congregation. Then, as bar/bat mitzvah planning approaches, grandparents, aunts, uncles, new wives, new husbands and new siblings suddenly spring forth, leaving the congregation's staff trying to play a quick game of "catch up" regarding a family's composition. Often, there is a growing sense of "crisis" which comes from not having had time to reflect on how to work toward including complex family segments in what can be a fairly straightforward religious celebration. A family's ability to address some of these issues in a timely and peaceful fashion can do much to pave the way for creative solutions to their predicaments.

How to Word Invitations

Wording reflects personal status and family configuration. Each family will have its own set of issues. Ideally, a workshop leader or a bar/bat mitzvah counselor will have a scrapbook of invitations available to show families so they can find not only the appropriate wording for their invitation, but also see many examples of what can be visually appealing invitations. Some examples:

An Invitation from the Bar/Bat Mitzvah Child

*"With great pleasure my family and I
Are delighted to invite you to join in our simcha as
I lead the congregation in prayer and
I am called to the Torah as a Bat Mitzvah"*

Sarah Cohen

An Invitation from Two Remarried Parents

*"We are delighted to invite you to share
with our families this joyous occasion when
our daughter
Sarah Cohen
will be called to the Torah as a Bat Mitzvah"*

Judy and Paul Schwartz
George* and Denise Cohen*

An Invitation from Parents Who Have Not Remarried or Have Decided Not to List the Names of New Spouses

*"We invite you to share in our happiness
when our daughter
Sarah Michelle
is called to the Torah as a Bat Mitzvah"*

Judy Cohen and George Cohen

---

* (Notice that the bat mitzvah girl's parents' names come first to signify that they are the bat mitzvah girl's parents)

"We invite you to share in our happiness
when our daughter
Sarah Michelle
is called to the Torah as a Bat Mitzvah"

Judy Cohen
George and Denise Cohen

THE BEAUTY — AND PAIN — OF PRESENTING THE *TALLIT*

This can be the most moving and most painful moment of the bar/bat mitzvah ceremony for divorced parents. Traditionally, it is a time for parents to pass on not only the *tallit*, but the memories of the hopes and expectations they had when their bar or bat mitzvah child was just a baby. For some families, it becomes a "This is your life!" For others, it is a moment in which to share the hopes and dreams of the past 13 years.

In most instances, mother and father present the *tallit* together, but some parents prefer to make statements to their bar or bat mitzvah child separately. After laboring for nine symbolic months to make a *tallit* for my daughter, for instance, I realized that I had woven my presentation to her into the threads of the *tallit*. My husband and I decided that I would present the *tallit* at the beginning of the service, and that he would share his thoughts as a proud Dad later in the service. We used the same format for our younger daughter's bat mitzvah three years later. Some people were surprised that we hadn't made a joint presentation, but it fit very comfortably into our family's style and into what we perceived as the purpose of the morning.

I offer the above example because it is important to share with families from the onset that there is rarely only one way to accomplish something, that even those traditions which appear to be etched in stone are, in fact, traditions and not *halachah* (Jewish law). It is *your* decision whether to make a joint presentation with your ex-spouse, and also whether to involve new spouses in the *tallit* presentation. However, if both parents commit to the bottom line that the bar or bat mitzvah celebration is *for your child,* the solution may become more readily apparent.

For some families, the pain of divorce is so intense that it is not emotionally possible to stand before the child and present a *tallit* which, for them, may expose the failed dreams of the family rather than the celebration of the child's achievements as a person. In these instances, it is important to share these feelings with the rabbi or bar/bat mitzvah teacher to figure out how to resolve this.

One family which participated in a support group program for divorced families approaching bar/bat mitzvah had exactly this dilemma. This was the family's third bar mitzvah celebration, but its first as a divorced family. The mother was afraid she would burst out crying if she had to say anything during the *tallit* presentation, yet she did not want to relinquish her position on the *bimah* during the presentation. We talked about the earlier bar mitzvah ceremonies in their family. The parents had stood together, but the father had made the actual presentation because the mother was afraid she would cry. Through this discussion, the couple decided that even though the mother's emotions were more complicated this time, choosing not to speak at this bar mitzvah ceremony would not be any different from her role at her other sons' bar mitzvah celebrations. This helped her set aside her self-consciousness about how the congregation might perceive her silence and she could stand beside her ex-husband, proudly sharing *as a parent* her son's receiving of the *tallit.*

Whom to Invite and Where to Seat Them

After our two daughters' b'not mitzvah celebrations, my husband and I joked that we needed a third bat mitzvah celebration to whom we could invite all those about whom we felt guilty for not inviting to the first two. All families struggle with invitation lists. Many factors go into compiling this list, all preceded by budget, budget and budget. In fact, no families can invite everyone they (a) *want* to invite and (b) feel they *ought* to invite.

The issue of a guest list is touchier when parents are divorced. There are often more budget constraints. Different tensions, too, arise among family members. One side of the family may simply fear that it will be uncomfortable to share a party with the divorced spouse's relatives. In another situation, family members may feel, rightly or wrongly, that something embarrassing might happen if the other side attends (for example, ex-family members refusing to greet each other civilly). At the extreme, there may be fears of screaming matches or insulting behavior between either the ex-spouses or members of their families.

These issues cause me particular concern when they are expressed by the child. I have had children tell me that they do not want their father's family invited because there might be terrible fights or arguments if both sides of the family are in the same room. They say they would be profoundly embarrassed in front of their peers should such behavior occur. Children need to be reassured that they will not be embarrassed by the behavior of family members toward one another — which means that the parents must assume responsibility for discussing these guidelines with any family members or guests who they suspect may have difficulty keeping their emotions in check.

Seating arrangements at the reception can often serve to limit social interaction in more difficult situations. One family that had experienced a particularly difficult divorce divided the room down the center: Father's family on the right, mother's family on the left. The son visited his mother's family tables with her, then visited the father's family tables with him. Neither parent visited each other's family tables.

If having a family "head table" is a problem, remember this: It is not written in stone that there must *be* a family head table. One family I know not only decided to abandon the head table, but used this as an opportunity to make *every* table at the reception an "A" table: Family members who normally would have been seated together were scattered to tables throughout the reception hall. As a result, each table became an "A" table because every table had a significant family member at it. Sometimes, adversity results in creative solutions from which all can benefit.

FOR EVERY FAMILY, THERE IS A "RIGHT" SOLUTION

You have been divorced and remarried for many years. Your ex-spouse recently remarried. You and your ex have shared custody, so your child has grown up with both of you. The divorce was not pleasant, but you have worked out fairly comfortable co-parenting arrangements and have maintained a respectable relationship with your former spouse's extended family. Your ex's new spouse, whom your child likes, will be at the bar mitzvah celebration, as will some of her family, since they all feel very close to your son. Question: How are all these people incorporated into the celebration?

A friend of mine, in a similar situation, collected videos of family *simchas* on the husband's side of the family. She showed them to her family, in order to help her son recognize people who would be at his bar mitzvah. This was a creative, very "1990s" method to introduce a child to the sudden appearance of a new extended family.

Can or should this new family be included in ways other than social, perhaps by appearing on the *bimah* with your ex-spouse? Or by being acknowledged at a candlelighting ceremony at the reception? These are certainly touchier areas. Again, your guideline: This is the *child's simcha*. Given this, the starting point for such a discussion is what such inclusion means to your child.

Remember, though, that children try to please both parents. Before you ask your child if it's all right to have your new husband standing next to your ex-husband, heed your instincts and think about what you know about your child. Children often clearly signal their concerns and worries about the family aspects of the bar/bat mitzvah event. Don't ask your child to give you permission to make a decision which you know will cause him or her discomfort. Put aside your preferences and act on the basis of what you know about your child. Never forget that *you* are the adult in this situation — and do not expect your child to be more mature than his or her parents!

For every family, there is a "right" solution. The task lies in carefully and sensitively discussing and negotiating these solutions, and remembering that this day marks your child's entry into adult Jewish life. Start with those issues which most readily lend themselves to solutions. You will find a growing sense of strength and empowerment as you discover solutions which seemed impossible are, indeed, within your grasp.

If you get "stuck," use whomever you are closest to at your congregation or among your friends to help you discuss these issues further. That is what a community is for. But most importantly: Enjoy and celebrate this wonderful *simcha*, knowing that how you resolve your family's unique issues will signal to your child that his or her family can move comfortably and competently into the next stage of life.

Making the Theme Meaningful

Rabbi Aaron Bergman

SOMEWHERE IN POLAND, 1944

My father celebrated his becoming bar mitzvah on a cattle train en route to a concentration camp. He was taken from his family home just a few days before the celebration was to have taken place. The presents had already been wrapped and the delicacies prepared when the Nazis came. My grandfather, at the risk of his own life, smuggled a bottle of wine onto the train in order to drink a *l'chaim* to my father. The remembrance of this loving act helped my father survive the war. At my own bar mitzvah reception in 1976, my father and I shared our own *l'chaim*. That moment continues to nourish me.

SOMEWHERE IN AMERICA, 1994

I have seen: A young man in a tuxedo lowered into a theater from the rafters while being accompanied by the theme from the James Bond movies. A young woman skating into the social hall on roller-skates to entertain her guests. A youth running into the room dribbling a soccer ball while a local professional soccer team trailed behind him. Scantily clad young men and women sitting lasciviously on the laps of friends while thundering music played.

Were they participating in Greek Week at a university? Were they the masters of ceremonies at a bacchanalia? No, they were guests at parties celebrating their becoming a bar or bat mitzvah. They were merely acting out the theme of the party.

PARTIES REFLECT CHILDREN'S PERSONALITIES AND PARENTS' PRIDE

Though my father's situation was extreme, it shows how powerful a parent's love for a child is. When we celebrate our children's becoming b'nai mitzvah in loving and appropriate ways, when even the party reflects our Jewish values, we provide them with the emotional tools they will need to become loving, giving Jews themselves.

That a party should have a theme for children becoming b'nai mitzvah is only a recent phenomenon. It is not necessarily a bad idea. Unfortunately, many vulgar activities that pass for "themes" are the result of our losing the connection between what the child does in the congregation — and the appropriate way of celebrating it. The party rarely reflects the fact that the child has assumed the obligation of the 613 Jewish commandments. This may be mentioned at a candlelighting ceremony, but just briefly. Rather, it is the "theme" that dominates the party from the decorations to the entertainment to the favors that guests take home.

Parents do not choose these themes at random. They want the party to reflect their child's personality, as well as their special qualities. Parents want to let the world know how precious their children are.

Rabbi Harold Kushner tells a wonderful story about Sid Luckman, a Jew who was a quarterback for the Chicago Bears. The first quarter of a big game was going very well. He completed his passes with little pressure from the defense. Things began to break down in the second quarter. Sid was chased all over the field by gigantic linebackers who would have liked nothing better than to separate his head from his shoulders. Suddenly, a voice came out of the stands: "It's OK Sidney, give them the ball. Your mother and I will get you a new one."

Jewish parents have great devotion, love and concern for their children. One of their wonderful qualities is their willingness to spend whatever is necessary for their children to be safe and happy. We want to provide them with everything we had — and more. We are grateful for their achievements and even dream that they will someday surpass us in having the comforts and pleasures of life.

When it comes time to plan the bar or bat mitzvah party, many parents feel that the more they spend on the party, the more people will know how much they love their child. This is a great source of anxiety and pressure, often leading to extraordinary extravagances. I do not think that people make these parties just to show off or that they are just looking for an excuse to make a fancy party. People do what they do because they have a deep, abiding love for their children.

THE COMMANDMENTS ARE THE THEME OF THE JEWISH PEOPLE

It sends a potent message to our children when friends and family fly in from all over the country (sometimes, indeed, from all over the world) to celebrate their accepting responsibility for the mitzvot. Children who see that much effort made on their behalf learn that they have great intrinsic worth. This sense of self-esteem, of knowing how much they are loved and cherished, can last — and enrich — a lifetime. Ultimately this aspect of the event has a deeper, more significant impact on the child than the party itself, no matter what the theme or level of extravagance. Indeed, it can leave meaningful memories long after the sweet table is closed, and the band goes home.

The very idea of celebrating a child's becoming obligated to keep the commandments is extraordinary, especially since we often look forward to rituals that release us *from* an obligation, such as a school graduation or retirement from a job. As adults, we often yearn to go back to our childhood in which we were responsible for no one but ourselves. We may accept our responsibilities as adults, but rarely feel joy for having done so.

It is our genius as a people that we rejoice in the law. The rabbis said that, at the age of thirteen, we could no longer use the folly of youth as an excuse for bad behavior. Nor could we blame our parents. Instead, we have our children proclaim their responsibilities in public — and then we throw a festive meal. Many in our society try to shift blame and remove personal responsibility and look at Jews as archaic or legalistic. I argue, though, that more than anything else, it is our loyalty to the Torah and the commandments that has sustained us to this day. *It is the commandments that are the theme of the Jewish people.*

Judaism would have died out completely if not for the commandments. Not just the ritual commandments (though they are certainly important), but especially those which require us to act lovingly toward others.

COMPASSION WILL OUTLAST THE PARTY

There is a beautiful story in the Talmud that takes place after the destruction of the Second Temple in Jerusalem. Rabban Yochanon Ben Zakkai was walking in Jerusalem with his student Rabbi Yehoshua following behind him. Rabbi Yehoshua saw the Temple in ruins. He said, "Woe is us for this destruction, for the destruction of the place that atoned for the sins of Israel." Rabban Yochanon said to him, "My child, there is no reason to make yourself so miserable. We have another kind of atonement that is just like it. It is *gemilut hasadim*, acts of lovingkindness. As God says in the Book of Hosea, 'It is kindness that I desire, not sacrifice.'"

This answer by Rabban Yochanon is one of the most revolutionary in Jewish history. He says that God is more concerned about how we treat each other than about God's own honor. Reaching the age of mitzvot, then, means more than having people pay a great deal of attention to our child. It means that our children have to start paying attention to the needs of others.

The parties celebrating our children becoming b'nai mitzvah must reflect this demand of God's for acts of lovingkindness. Parents and children can pick a favorite cause to work toward and share the results with their guests. The guests themselves can be asked to involve themselves with the family's cause as a tribute to the family. The bat or bar mitzvah could — and should — deliver a few words of Torah on the importance of compassion for others.

The commandments, though, are more than a way of helping others. They are a way to help ourselves, to feel connected to Jews all over the world today and in our past. This is the great value of the Jewish ritual commandments. Ritual is a vessel for conveying memories. When we light candles on *Shabbat*, we stand with one hundred generations of Jews before us. When we wrap *tefillin*, we bring to life and bind ourselves to those Jews who first put them on two thousand years ago. When we pray, we speak the same words and dream the same dreams as our brothers and sisters from the Middle Ages and in every country in the world. This, too, is a theme of the bat and bar mitzvah party.

God has given us a great gift in the commandments. I hope that we and our families will always make them the theme of our lives, which will be enriched by them. May they take us from strength to strength.

Do You Need a Party Planner?

Cantor Helen Leneman

Party planners are sometimes blamed for the stress that is often placed on the bar/bat mitzvah party and which may over-shadow the religious component of the event. But while party planners' poor reputations may have originated with that by now hackneyed phrase, "too much bar, not enough mitzvah," the bar or bat mitzvah party is an integral part of a child's becoming bar or bat mitzvah in contemporary America. And having a party to cele-brate accomplishment need not detract from the *meaning* of becom-ing a bar or bat mitzvah. Joy and pride on having attained this milestone are accompanied by relief that the hardest part is over and by a desire to celebrate this joyously and festively.

What Can a Party Planner Do for You?

For personal, philosophical or financial reasons, some families choose not to use a party planner. For others, this person is the key to a successful celebration. Party planners can be expected to do some or all of the following: During the planning stages, they help you find a location for your party; suggest caterers and menus; order yarmulkes imprinted with the name of your child and the date of the event; advise you on choosing invitations and a printer, and remind you when to order and mail them. For the party itself, the party planner may provide everything for the party but the food; set up the reception room and time the sequence of the whole event — the cocktail reception, lunch, dancing, and candlelighting ceremony; and put all the gifts, centerpieces and any articles left on tables into carts for you to pick up as you leave the party.

HOW TO SELECT A PARTY PLANNER

If you decide to hire a party planner, thoroughly investigate the company you are considering. Inquire about its background and how its personnel got into the field. Many party planners do not have professional training for this work. Some are women who planned their own child's bar or bat mitzvah party, found they had a knack for it, and decided to go into the field professionally. Professional training could include degrees in banquet and catering or in the hotel field, though party planners without this background can still meet your needs, depending on your requirements and their area of expertise.

After determining the party planner's background, make sure that what you are paying for is very clear and in writing. For example, many planners will not stay and run the affair itself because they aren't qualified to. They may have an artistic flair, and enjoy making sign-in boards and centerpieces, but they actually subcontract the rest of the work. This may add a third-person fee to their rates. The amount of this fee will vary widely, depending on how much of the work your party planner is contracting out. Hiring a professional party planner who custom-makes everything without subcontracting eliminates this extra fee.

Customized party decorations involve training and experience. A "balloon college" is held every year for professional party planners so they can update their skills. Balloons have literally become a million-dollar business and the 1994 balloon seminar was even broadcast live on CNN.

Other decorating skills are: Lighting design, detonating balloons (for which a license is required), working with fabrics, and creating balloon sculptures, such as a 20-foot jukebox sculpted out of balloons.

In addition to knowing your party planner's background and laying out his or her responsibilities, it is important to feel comfortable and have a good rapport with whomever you hire. Using a party planner you trust alleviates stress, especially if you let them shoulder full responsibility for the party. Party planners are also responsible for rescuing you in an emergency. For example, if the bus chartered to take the children from the synagogue to the party does not show up, the party planner will be responsible for recruiting drivers from the adults present to transport the children.

STAYING WITHIN A BUDGET

Upon first meeting your family, a party planner will ask what kind of party you want, where it will be held, at what time of day, and the size of your budget. A good party planner will detail every item on the budget, whose overall amount families need to decide at the outset of planning.

A party planner can help you even if you have a fairly limited budget. Keep in mind that there are many variables in the cost of your party. For example, the number of guests, the type of entertainment, the photographer, the type of luncheon and the amount of alcohol consumed. The possible per-person cost of a luncheon event can range from $20 to $85. To save money, a planner might suggest renting such items as a centerpiece; renting a hall and bringing in your own caterer, rather than holding the party in a restaurant or using a facility's on-site caterers (depending on the amount and type of food you request, a caterer can often save you money); or having a deli luncheon, which is always reasonably priced.

BALANCING YOUR WISHES — AND YOUR CHILD'S

Because this event is costly, parents sometimes forget that it is still the child's party. As at least one girl has asked her mother, "Whose bat mitzvah is this, mine or yours?" Families should make some decisions together about the party before meeting with the party planner.

Party planners can help you achieve a balance between your child's wishes, your own standards and your budget. The key element of a successful party is good entertainment. If klezmer music is the parents' first choice, and the child wants contemporary dance music, klezmer could be featured during the cocktail hour, but not at the party. The event should be neither exclusively an adult party nor a teen party. However, if a band is hired that is not suitable for children, they may get bored and restless.

Party planners stay informed about the newest ideas for parties, such as placing disposable cameras on adults' tables with a message on a card, such as:

> "Though at performances, flashes are not allowed,
> since it's annoying for the performers and the crowd,
> on Jesse's very special day,
> pick up a camera and feel free to snap away."

The idea is that adults will photograph one another and leave the camera behind. Another option is to show a video during the party (either professionally done or homemade) of the bar or bat mitzvah child's life.

Since 90 percent of families want a theme for their party, a party planner can suggest possibilities. While Jewish themes, of course, are popular, families frequently choose themes unrelated to Judaism but specific to their child's interests, such as sports and hobbies. The theme should be a way for children to express their identity, not their parents'. Unfortunately, too often the parents, not the children, pick the theme.

Many parents host extravagant parties to impress their friends and business associates without considering the message they're sending their children. This can escalate in a particular community: Each family may try to equal or top the last party. A good party planner will help you resist this kind of pressure by pointing out that a party's success is not directly proportional to the amount of money spent, and will help keep the focus on the child. The child, after all, worked for this day and earned the party — even if *you* paid for it. The party should be a place for the child to express his or her identity, where adults and children can share equally in a joyous celebration they will remember fondly the rest of their lives.

COMING OF AGE

THE SIGNIFICANCE OF BAR/BAT MITZVAH FOR INTERFAITH FAMILIES

Joan C. Hawxhurst

The decision to have a bar/bat mitzvah ceremony is often an automatic one for families with two Jewish parents, but for families with parents of two different faiths the decision must be more conscious and thoughtful. In fact, according to sociologist Egon Mayer of the Jewish Outreach Institute in New York, only about 15 percent of the children in interfaith families go through the bar or bat mitzvah ceremony.

No matter what their initial opinions about this ceremony, interfaith families should spend time discussing each family member's feelings about having a bar or bat mitzvah ceremony. Both parents and the adolescent child may have different reasons for considering a bar/bat mitzvah, and all of these need to be acknowledged so the family can determine how to proceed.

It is especially important that interfaith families take a fresh look at what it means to "come of age." Coming-of-age is the one life cycle event in which a family's composition doesn't change. There is no birth or death; no new family is created. The change is, thus, more subtle and less immediate, but potentially profound as well.

"If you understand coming-of-age as a passage, a process of transition from one stage to another," suggests Hugh Sanborn, a pastoral therapist in Houston, Texas, "then it becomes clear that a

151

coming-of-age service is not intended to be a completion, as though adolescence ends one day and young adulthood begins the next. Rather, it celebrates the changes that are taking place in the life of the young adult and the parents." It is these changes, and how they are interpreted by family members, that will shape decisions about having a bar/bat mitzvah ceremony.

On top of the many challenges facing teenagers in the United States today, teenagers in Jewish-Christian families must somehow come to terms with their distinctive religious identities. "The job of the adolescent is to question, challenge and begin to develop independent reasoning abilities," psychotherapist Joel Crohn writes in *Mixed Matches: How to Create Successful Interracial, Interethnic, and Interfaith Marriages*. "In single-religion homes, adolescents will tend to identify with parents' beliefs. In homes with two religions or no clear religion, the adolescent will often either reject religion entirely or choose one as 'the best.'" Crohn suggests that "each child's path through the process of creating an identity is unique, and all involve a process of experimentation and change."

Crohn acknowledges that children's struggles to understand their complex identities can be quite difficult for their parents: "We can guide our children, teach them, and expose them to the cultural and religious worlds we hope they will embrace. But no matter how carefully we orchestrate our children's experiences, as they approach adulthood, we can never control or predict how they will identify. Just as we have broken with some of the traditions and ways of our parents and ancestors, so, too, will our children create change with the new world they are helping to create."

ENRICHING THE CHILD, ENRICHING OURSELVES

If interfaith parents can understand and respect the identity struggle their child may be experiencing, the work of planning a meaningful coming-of-age ceremony will be easier. Parents — Jewish *and* Christian — of interfaith adolescents must also ask themselves how much of the ceremony they are planning is designed to help them with their own issues, and how much it will benefit and enrich the child. "After birth," writes Susan Weidman Schneider in *Intermarriage: The Challenge of Living with Differences Between Christians and Jews*, "there are a few other ceremonial occasions that provide opportunities for the interfaith couple to express how they're raising their children and what their goals are for them." She suggests that coming-of-age rituals for an adolescent are difficult for a family to navigate because "the religious aspects of the ritual obviously have an intellectual impact on him or her that the birth ceremonies did not."

There are certain ways that an interfaith family can help the non-Jewish parent and extended family feel welcome and included in what may feel to them like a foreign ritual. An interfaith family can offer to its non-Jewish extended family (in a letter, a phone call, or in person) an explanation of the meaning and rituals of the bar/bat mitzvah ceremony. And certain elements can be incorporated into the service itself to assure that the non-Jewish spouse feels included, such as a non-Jewish parent's favorite poem.

Sometimes it is the child who asks for a bar or bat mitzvah in an interfaith family that has not decided to be either Jewish or Christian. This was the case with Paul Rosenbloom, of Palo Alto, California, who was raised with both Presbyterian and Jewish influences. "Some time during the seventh grade," he remembers, "I started to get a nagging thought in the back of my head, that I wanted to have a bar mitzvah." Paul's desire grew out of the inadequacy he felt regarding Judaism: "I felt like an outsider. I wanted to familiarize myself with Judaism. I was tired of being so uncomfortable about such a basic part of myself." At his initiative, Paul and his Jewish father worked together to fashion a meaningful, comfortable bar mitzvah ceremony and celebration.

Affirming Identity

More often, it is the Jewish parent who suddenly realizes that he or she deems it important to have a child become bar/bat mitzvah. The authors of *The Intermarriage Handbook*, Judy Petsonk and Jim Remsen, contend that Jewish parents are more likely than Christian parents to push for their own faith's coming-of-age ceremony: "The Christian ceremony is a statement of faith. Many of the Christian partners we talked to had lost their faith years earlier. They saw no particular reason to ask their children to make declarations of Christian faith. The Jewish ceremony, however, affirms identification with a people. The Jewish partner may have no faith, yet still identify as a Jew. He or she wants his or her child to share in that identification." Perhaps this is the primary reason that many Jewish parents want their children, whom they had essentially raised as products of an interfaith environment, to experience the bar/bat mitzvah ceremony.

Unfortunately, many interfaith families do nothing to mark their children's rite of passage. Until now, the majority of Jewish-Christian families have let their children's adolescent years slip by without a concrete coming-of-age marker. In a world largely bereft of guideposts for teenagers who must face increasingly difficult moral and ethical decisions early in their lives, this is a shame. As interfaith families become more numerous and more comfortable straddling two religious worlds, they may choose to be more conscious about marking important transitions in their family lives. The bar/bat mitzvah ceremony may thus become one of a number of increasingly acceptable alternatives chosen by interfaith families.

Celebrating Bar/Bat Mitzvah Successfully as an Interfaith Family

Lena Romanoff

A bar or bat mitzvah ceremony is a rite of passage that happens to a family, not just to an individual child. It can be a time of inspiration, comfort, joy and celebration — or it can be stressful and filled with tension.

During transition times and life cycle events, individuals seek the comfort and familiarity of their cultural and religious traditions as frames of reference to guide them through the changes. An interfaith couple may face problems when a shared life cycle event, such as the birth of a child or selecting a child's religious education, is viewed with different significance, symbols and rituals. The religious identity of the children is a monumental — and sometimes impossible — decision for parents to make. Parents, family and friends who attempt to offer advice may increase divisions of loyalty, confusion, hostility and tensions. Ultimately, the decision must be made by the parents, who want to do the "right" thing for their children and avoid hurting or confusing them.

Under ideal circumstances, interfaith couples discussed their ethnic, cultural, and religious differences before marriage and openly communicated their concerns and conflicts. By learning about each other's religion and carefully re-examining their own, they should hopefully be able to decide on the religious identity and educational upbringing of their children.

My experience in counseling thousands of interfaith families on these choices and conflicts has convinced me that children ultimately do best when raised in a warm, unified one-faith household, even when the conversion of a parent has not occurred. Some parents attempt to raise their children in two faiths simultaneously. This may work well for the parents but not for the children, even if problems or concerns may not be evident when children are young. On the surface, these children would seem to have the best of the Christian and Jewish worlds. As they get older, they begin to focus on the messages behind the holidays and rituals. When theological differences begin to be explored, many parents find themselves at a loss for the right answers. If God alone is divine, what is Jesus? Can I receive communion and still become bar or bat mitzvah? Must I believe in Jesus to have salvation? What should I believe about death and life after death? Will we all be together when we die? Which part of me is Jewish? Which is Christian? To whom do I pray? Which religion is really "right," Mom's or Dad's? *Who am I?*

When the gentile partner agrees to raise the children as Jews, the Jewish community should recognize the magnitude and significance of this decision: The gentile parent is unselfishly giving up the right to raise the child in his or her own faith (and in the dominant culture) and is willing to be either a passive or active participant in having the child raised as a Jew. This does not mean that the gentile partner should not share other aspects of him or herself with the child. Quite the opposite! This partner should share his or her cultural and ethnic background, experiences and memories, as well as explain his or her own religious beliefs. And the Jewish partner must be alert to the needs of the gentile partner. When a couple decides to raise the child as a Jew, the gentile partner must feel that his or her needs have been fully considered.

INVOLVING NON-JEWISH RELATIVES

The primary concern of the non-Jewish family is that they will not be a part of their grandchild's (or niece's or nephew's) life.

However, closeness between the bar or bat mitzvah child and the Christian grandparents can be achieved by having them work on a family album, a genealogical tree or some form of family history. The interfaith couple should buy the Christian family a Jewish calendar when the children are small to help the grandparents familiarize themselves with the holidays and rituals. And at all times, the Christian family should respect the couple's religious boundaries and prerogatives.

By the time children are of bar or bat mitzvah age, most concerns about raising them as Jews have been resolved and accepted — or at least tolerated. Some families avoid religious issues and do not share holidays because this might lead to angry words and the opening of old wounds. The interfaith couple is then faced with the dilemma of what to do about the bar/bat mitzvah celebration. Families should work hard to maintain communication and look for common bonds to strengthen their ties.

Regardless of the relationship, most Christian relatives appreciate an invitation accompanied by a personal letter from the parents and child, requesting their presence at the bar or bat mitzvah ceremony. This way, the decision to attend is left to the relative. If they decide not to attend, it may be disappointing, but their decision should be respected. Neither angry words nor reminders of past hurts will change the decision and will only cast a dark cloud on what should be a bright event.

KNOW YOUR CONGREGATION'S POLICIES ABOUT INTERFAITH BAR/BAT MITZVAH

Before joining a congregation (which should occur several years before your child turns 13), find out the congregation's policy on the Jewish identity of children of interfaith marriages. I have had the heartbreaking task of trying to comfort children who were raised as Conservative Jews, yet were denied a bar/bat mitzvah ceremony because the gentile mother had not converted to Judaism before her child's birth or the child had not converted. Usually, the problems are solved by having the child convert. However, many hurt, humiliated and angry children have refused to convert. It is devastating to a child who feels, thinks and acts Jewishly to be told that he or she is not a "real" Jew. This scenario can be avoided by asking the right questions before joining a congregation or before beginning your child's Jewish education, and certainly long before the bar or bat mitzvah ceremony.

If you do belong to a congregation, inquire well in advance of the bar/bat mitzvah date about the role of the non-Jewish partner and non-Jewish family in the service. Ask how the congregation's policies or regulations affect your interfaith family. For instance, if a child is raised as a Reform Jew and receives a formal Jewish education, the child is considered Jewish by the Reform movement even if one parent is not Jewish. However, almost no rabbi will let a child have a bar/bat mitzvah ceremony if the child is receiving formal religious education in another faith while attending Hebrew school.

MAKE SURE THE NON-JEWISH SPOUSE FULLY PARTICIPATES

Once the family has decided to have a bar or bat mitzvah ceremony, the Jewish parent should take the leading role in the preparations, since the gentile partner may feel overwhelmed by all the strange preparations, rules and traditions. But do include your partner in all the decision making.

Many children worry that their non-Jewish parent will feel left out of their bar/bat mitzvah celebration — or, worse, that the parent may not *want* to be part of it or is even against it. Your child needs the love, attention, and support of both parents. Sometimes taking your child to weekly lessons with the tutor, encouraging him or her during practice for the bar/bat mitzvah service, or helping the child choose clothes for the event can be the greatest support a parent can provide. If this comes from the gentile parent, it makes a particularly strong statement to the child.

Even if the gentile parent does not fully agree about the child having a bar/bat mitzvah ceremony, it is not fair to your child for the partner to remain visibly angry once the decision has been made. If the gentile partner agreed reluctantly to the bar/bat mitzvah and later becomes too upset to participate or support it in any way, any lingering resentment should be kept private. No emotional or loyalty obstacles should be put in the way of your child's bar or bat mitzvah. Family unity and togetherness are crucial to the child.

KEEP YOUR NON-JEWISH IN-LAWS INFORMED

Preparing for a bar or bat mitzvah celebration means preparing not only the child and his or her family, but also the non-Jewish family. This is done by telling the gentile family what they can expect, and, when possible, involving them in the preparations for the celebration. Many non-Jewish families may not want to participate in the religious aspects of the service, but may prefer to help with tasks related to the celebration, such as the guest list or shopping for party favors.

Become familiar with your congregation's rules and regulations. Can the non-Jewish family participate by reading English sections of the service, reciting the *shehecheyanu* blessing, or offering a few personal words? Will the gentile parent be allowed to participate, or will he or she be a passive observer? Will the gentile parent be allowed on the *bimah*? How does the bar/bat mitzvah child feel about the roles his or her parents, family and friends have at the ceremony?

While the service may not permit too much personal creativity, the celebration can lend itself to all sorts of personalization. For instance, the music and food chosen can reflect the ethnic backgrounds of both sets of parents. At the same time, remember that a rabbi or family members who observe the laws of *kashrut* will not be able to eat at your affair unless you make special provisions for them.

Many non-Jews have never attended a bar or bat mitzvah or any other synagogue service and may be uncomfortable. Many couples prepare a brochure or booklet that welcomes their guests and provides basic explanations of the rituals that will take place, along with advice such as the fact that non-Jews should not wear a *tallit* but may wear a yarmulke. Transliterations of the Hebrew used in the service should be provided wherever possible. The key word in all of this is planning. There are as many different solutions as there are families. With good planning, you will achieve the maximum benefits for your entire family, both Jewish and non-Jewish.

Michael Becomes Bar Mitzvah

The Story of a Special Needs Child

Beverly Weaver

When he was two years old, he spoke in complete sentences. But his behavior was so impulsive that the china closet had to be bolted to the wall to prevent him from pulling it over.

When he was five years old, he could whistle Beethoven concerti. But when asked, "What is one plus one?" he replied "Give me a hint!"

When he entered fifth grade, he did not know multiplication tables, but he could (and did) cook an entire Thanksgiving dinner, making everything from scratch — including stuffing, cranberry sauce, and several varieties of pie.

When he was thirteen years old, he had a bar mitzvah ceremony. A perfect bar mitzvah ceremony.

This is a story of how one learning disabled boy and his family had a very positive bar mitzvah experience. If you are the parent of a child with any type of learning disability, I hope this story gives you insight into the frustrations and problems of the learning disabled student as well as a few strategies for coping with the kinds of difficult learning disabled situations which you and your child face on a daily basis. I hope you also have a good laugh as you recognize the scenarios described.

TACKLING THE DECISION

Our son Michael was identified as learning disabled at the age of four. When he was in the fifth grade, school was a daily struggle and coping with homework was even worse. Coping with Hebrew school was beyond worse. Yet, in spite of all, he was a great, funny child with special talents and abilities. When we got a letter from our congregation inviting us to a meeting to assign bar/bat mitzvah dates for Michael's Hebrew school class, it dawned on us that this wonderful child would be facing the pressures of bar mitzvah training before we knew it and that we needed to plan for it. I don't mean we started to call caterers and listen to bands, but that we consciously decided that we wanted our son's bar mitzvah memories to be pleasant. And we believed that this would not happen unless we planned for it to happen.

The philosophy of the rabbi and the director of religious education at our Conservative congregation was that bar/bat mitzvah study was designed to lead teenagers into observant adulthood. Consequently, bar/bat mitzvah students learned, among other things, to chant Friday night services, Saturday morning *Shacharit*, Torah, and *Musaf* services; the trope for both *Haftarah* and Torah; *aliyah Haftarah* blessings; their own *Haftarah* and Torah portions; and English translations of their *Haftarah* and Torah portions so they can prepare discussions about them. The congregation's teenage population was small enough that there was no need for pairing b'nai mitzvah at the ceremony, so the glory — and the pressure — of the day all fell on one person. On the other hand, both the rabbi and the religious education director made it well known that, halachically, a boy is bar mitzvah when he turns thirteen and is automatically obligated to the mitzvot, whether or not he has a bar mitzvah ceremony; that bar mitzvah is not a contest between students, and though pre-bar mitzvah study was non-negotiable, some aspects of the bar mitzvah ceremony were, including having a bar mitzvah service in Israel.

THE INITIAL DECISION: LET MICHAEL CHOOSE

The first decision we made was that Michael should choose the bar mitzvah option comfortable for him, even if he chose not to have a bar mitzvah ceremony. I recalled that, several years earlier when I was the Sisterhood's catering vice-president, I helped parents plan the *Kiddush* events for their children's bar/bat mitzvah ceremonies. One day, a mother called one month before the date set for her son's bar mitzvah ceremony to tell me that the ceremony had been re-scheduled for the next year because her son was learning disabled and could not be ready in time. The family moved shortly after their son's bar mitzvah ceremony, and I never learned how the boy felt about celebrating his special day one year later than planned. But I did know that my own son was sensitive to the differences his learning disabled problems presented and (rightly or wrongly) would be embarrassed by such a change in scheduling his bar mitzvah celebration.

THE SECOND DECISION: LET MICHAEL BE TREATED THE SAME AS OTHERS

The next decision we made was that, if Michael had a bar mitzvah ceremony at the synagogue, it would take place as scheduled and with his bar/bat mitzvah class.

I recalled Michael telling me tearfully one day: "I'm so tired of being different. Just once I wish I could be like everyone else." So we also decided that his bar mitzvah ceremony would not be noticeably different from anyone else's.

THE LAST DECISION: MAKE IT POSITIVE

The final experience occurred as a result of contact with a cousin whom we had not seen in twenty years. In the course of relating family stories, he shared a poignant story about his younger brother, whose learning disability had not been diagnosed when he was a child. This, of course, had interfered with bar mitzvah training. Our cousin still had a bar mitzvah practice tape which had been made for his brother, on which the cantor could be heard screaming in the background. Even with all the practicing (and screaming), David could not learn a *Haftarah* portion or the Saturday morning service. He ended up doing only the *aliyah* blessings. To this day, he cringes at the memories of the entire experience. So the final decision we made was that our son's bar mitzvah experience would be something positive that he could store in his heart and carry into his Jewish future.

A FULL COMMITMENT FROM MICHAEL

My husband and I thought it best to discuss these matters with Michael privately. No siblings allowed. So, two years ahead of the bar mitzvah year, the three of us went for a walk to discuss an event for which we didn't even have a date. We told Michael that the decision rested solely with him, and we would not be disappointed if he chose not to have a bar mitzvah ceremony at thirteen — or ever. We loved him and respected him and knew how hard he worked to keep up in school. If bar mitzvah study was one thing too many for him to do, that was fine with us: He was still a good Jew and a great son. This was not something he needed to do for us. However, if he chose to have a bar mitzvah ceremony, he had to agree to work hard and to see it through to the end. Tougher yet, there could be no daily complaints about the workload.

Those were tough conditions for a pre-teen boy to accept, and we knew it. But we would accept no less. If we were going to put in two years of work, it simply could not be a daily fight, and it should not be in vain.

Not surprising to us, Michael quickly ruled out having no bar mitzvah ceremony, as well as having one in Israel, which was too different from what his friends were doing. He worried over a bar mitzvah ceremony at the synagogue, but chose to do it because being different was not desirable at this stage in his life. Michael, who has always had a strong work ethic, readily agreed to try to learn as much of the bar mitzvah curriculum as possible. My husband and I sweetened the pot with the promise of a Saturday night party for Michael and his friends.

HELPING SMOOTH THE WAY

Later that night, my husband and I decided that I would essentially manage the bar mitzvah study plan since I professionally tutor learning disabled students. Michael always says that his learning problems are like speed bumps: They slow him down, but don't stop him cold. My first job was to figure out how many of those speed bumps currently stood between him and a successful bar mitzvah ceremony.

The next day, I went to work. I had observed that although the bar/bat mitzvah curriculum was all-inclusive for study, there was some variance in what each child actually did at his or her bar/bat mitzvah ceremony. Few did the entire Friday night service, and many did not do *Shacharit* on Saturday or read all the Torah portions. On the other hand, almost everyone did the Torah service and *Musaf* and the *Maftir* Torah portion. And, everyone did his or her *Haftarah* (including the blessings before and after), *aliyah* blessings, a Torah and *Haftarah* discussion and a personal speech. I concluded that Michael could concentrate on what everyone (or almost everyone) did and still have a bar mitzvah ceremony acceptable to him. I listed every selection in the Torah service and *Musaf* service and had Michael try to chant each one. Next to each I noted whether Michael could reliably chant it. That list helped me understand how much had yet to be taught to him. After that, I pored over the *chumash* and listed every *Haftarah* portion and how many verses were in each. I highlighted those with the fewest verses. Then I met privately with our rabbi and education director, and told them that I was not looking for an easy way out for my son, but a viable path to a successful bar mitzvah ceremony for a special needs child. Together, we chose a *Haftarah* of just thirteen sentences, which also was an available *Shabbat* on the calendar.

DETOURING AROUND THE DISABILITY

Bar mitzvah speed bump number one was cleared. Reality replaced guesswork. I now knew the workload and the target date. Unfortunately, speed bump number two was more of a hurdle. Both the services and the *Haftarah* were in Hebrew — not a surprise in a Conservative congregation, but still a formidable problem considering the fact that Michael had never learned to reliably read Hebrew. Since Hebrew is written with consonants on top of vowels, it requires some visual integration to read even the most simple Hebrew word. Michael's learning disability blocked him from integrating those images. The only way he could read Hebrew was to read the consonant to himself and remember it, read the vowel to himself and remember it; then orally combine them. This was a painfully slow, often inaccurate process. But, I knew that time and knowledge were on my side: I had a full two years for focused study and I knew that Michael was a good auditory learner. With a plan and a learning strategy, speed bump number two was looking less formidable.

SETTING REALISTIC GOALS

To successfully manage the time component, I made a "rigidly flexible" schedule. I roughly divided the months between the current date and the bar mitzvah date into thirds, with the last third slightly larger than the other two. The first time span would be devoted to studying the Torah service, the second time span would be devoted to studying *Musaf*, and the third time span would be devoted to studying *Haftarah*. One month was set aside at the end for review and working on the speeches. If things went faster than planned, we could add a *maftir* Torah portion at the end. If things went slower than planned, the review month would give us time to re-group.

Michael and I worked together five out of almost every seven days for two years (minus vacations). That was the rigid part: Making sure we kept to a schedule. The flexible part was that we varied the days and amount of time spent each day according to my son's wishes and needs: His mood, his secular school work load, and we never worked on vacations. On the best days, we worked as long as 30 to 45 minutes. On not-so-good days, we worked as few as 5 to 10 minutes. On days when Michael felt more relaxed, we worked on something new. On less relaxed days, we reviewed work already learned.

At first, I set the days and the time of day for studying. But Michael grumbled if he was interrupted from something else. So we compromised. As long as he chose five days out of every seven, he could select the day and time and even change it daily, just as long as he did not pick an entirely inappropriate time, such as when I was making dinner or had other commitments.

Making good use of my knowledge of learning strategies was tougher than scheduling. By definition, an auditory learner usually gets more information when it is explained orally than when it is read silently. I had initially assumed that Michael could learn everything for bar mitzvah by listening to a tape. But, I quickly found that he needed more input than just his ears. The information was too unfamiliar to master with only one sense. So, by trial and error, we eventually found that listening to a tape and mastering each selection was most effective. Then I taught it to Michael, in very small doses, using a multi-sensory approach: Michael listened to me sing (auditory input) while he looked at the written page (visual input) and followed along with his finger touching each word (tactile input).

TEMPERS AND DOOR-SLAMMING

This worked because it set realistic goals and gave Michael a say in its operation. But it did not all go smoothly. There were some real book-slamming, door-slamming, "I can't do this!" "Yes, you can!" frustrations. One difficulty occurred each time we started something new. Michael would often be sulky and demanding ("You're singing too fast, too slowly, too loudly...I'm tired, thirsty, bored, etc."). Once I recognized this pattern, I explained it to Michael, and he tried not to let it happen again. But, I think he truly dreaded beginning each new selection. It was like mythical Sisyphus continually pushing that boulder up the hill only to have it fall back down each time he got to the top.

Once, I slammed the prayer book shut and made Michael take a walk with me to clear the air. We started out with me in the lead, furiously walking and pumping my arms as fast as I could. Michael did the same, but made sure not to give me the satisfaction of walking with me: He was about half a block behind. As I cooled down and slowed down, the next thing I knew he was walking with me. After awhile, we actually talked to each other; by the time we got home, we both felt okay. We decided maybe walking was a pretty good tension reliever. I didn't keep track of how many times we resorted to that, but I know I lost five pounds without dieting that summer!

When I mentioned to others what I was doing with Michael, their common response was always surprise that I would tutor my own son for bar mitzvah. But, I never saw myself as Michael's tutor. I was the bar mitzvah facilitator. My goal was not to bypass the religious school's bar/bat mitzvah program, but to prepare Michael well enough so that he could participate in that program. Sometimes, this method is called pre-teaching. It involves giving a learning disabled student information at a slower speed and with a method more appropriate for him to learn so that he becomes familiar enough with the information to "get it" when it is taught in class.

First Steps Towards Independence

A month before his bar mitzvah ceremony, Michael had satisfactorily completed everything on our initial list. I resisted the bar/bat mitzvah class teacher's idea that Michael add either *Shacharit* service or Torah reading. Michael seemed comfortable with what he had already learned, but my instincts told me that he had "maxed out." I have seen overloaded learning disabled students "lose" knowledge as unexpectedly and completely as a computer whose hard disk crashes, and I concentrated on repetition and relaxation during those last weeks.

Then it happened. Michael walked into the sanctuary one *Shabbat* morning. Sometime about mid-morning he put on a *tallit* and flawlessly led the congregation in prayer and study as though it was the easiest and most natural task in the world. Nothing will ever be quite the same again. That day really did mark the first step towards Michael's independence from his father and me. He had a bar mitzvah service, a successful one with good memories. A *perfect* bar mitzvah ceremony.

PROLOGUE

Our next son just got his bar mitzvah date. It will be two years from now. He asked me the other day when we would start studying together. Since he has no learning difficulties, I said I had not planned to do extra work with him. I had assumed that he would want to take the routine bar mitzvah study course at the synagogue, and not do so much extra work at home. But he responded, "For two years, I watched you and Michael go upstairs, close the bedroom door and have that time all to yourselves. I want that, too." So, here we go: Bar mitzvah times two!

On the Learning Path

Selected Resources for Parents

Compiled by Dr. Barbara Wachs

The following list of books deals with topics of interest to families preparing for bar/bat mitzvah. Included are books about different aspects of bar/bat mitzvah, children's books about bar/bat mitzvah, Jewish parenting books, books to guide families in Torah study, and videos which can be viewed together by families to stimulate further exploration into the meaning of this event.

Many of these books can be found in your public or congregation's library or in the library of your local Board of Jewish Education or Jewish Community Center. They can also be purchased at a Jewish book store or at a large general book store. The videos may be found in a Board of Jewish Education library; a few can be found in a video rental store.

"I'D LIKE TO READ MORE BOOKS ABOUT BAR/BAT MITZVAH TRADITIONS AND PRACTICES."

Diamond, Barbara. *Bat Mitzvah: A Jewish Girl's Coming of Age.* New York: Viking Press, 1995.

Well-written treasure trove of information about Jewish women's history and contemporary bat mitzvah practices. Covers services and celebrations. Contains a useful glossary of Hebrew terms and a section where bat mitzvah girls reflect on their experiences.

Efron, Benjamin and Alvan D. Rubin. *Coming of Age: Your Bar/Bat Mitzvah.* New York: Union of American Hebrew Congregations, 1977.

Reform Judaism's perspective on bar/bat mitzvah. Aimed at students, but also useful to parents. A basic introduction to the history, rituals and significance of the bar/bat mitzvah ceremony. Provides excellent background material and deals with student concerns.

Eisenberg, Azriel Louis. *Bar Mitzvah Treasury*. West Orange, N.J.: Behrman House, 1956.

Anthology of essays on topics of interest to the bar mitzvah. The bar mitzvah stories from different places and times are recommended.

Isaacs, Ronald H. and Kerry M. Olitzky. *Doing Mitzvot: Mitzvah Projects for Bar/Bat Mitzvah*. New York: KTAV, 1994.

For bar/bat mitzvah students and their families. Includes 12 mitzvot, one for each month of the year: ten mitzvot *ben adam lehavero* (interpersonal mitzvot) and two mitzvot *ben adam lamakom* (mitzvot between people and God). Each chapter contains original sources, questions to think about, research topics, suggested projects, a mitzvah diary and a bibliography.

Kimmel, Eric A. *Bar Mitzvah: A Jewish Boy's Coming of Age*. New York: Viking Press, 1995.

Historical background, explanations of ceremonial objects and rituals, and real-life bar mitzvah stories. Suitable for a boy preparing for his ceremony or for anyone who wants to learn about this tradition.

Lewit, Jane and Ellen Robinson Epstein. *Bar/Bat Mitzvah Planbook*. Chelsea, Mich.: Scarborough House, 1991.

Useful information about choosing dates, preparing your child, choosing invitations, appropriate gifts, alternative celebrations, parties, *tzedakah*. Many helpful charts and timetables.

Lipstadt, Deborah E. "Bar/Bat Mitzvah" in the *Second Jewish Catalogue*. Philadelphia: Jewish Publication Society, 1976.

A chapter on bar/bat mitzvah emphasizing customs, alternative celebrations and special activities for the pre- and post- bar/bat mitzvah year.

Reisfeld, Randi. *The Bar/Bat Mitzvah Survival Guide.* New York: Citadel Press, 1992.

Practical, lighthearted, informative look at the bar/bat mitzvah celebration. Explanations of major costs and hidden expenses. Money-saving tips and a complete chart for tracking expenses.

Rossel, Seymour. *A Spiritual Journey: The Bar and Bat Mitzvah Handbook.* West Orange, N.J.: Behrman House, 1993.

Answers basic questions about bar/bat mitzvah ritual. Designed for students and parents. Clear, concise question-answer format.

Salkin, Jeffrey K. *Putting God on the Guest List: How to Reclaim the Spiritual Meaning of Your Child's Bar or Bat Mitzvah.* Woodstock, Vt.: Jewish Lights Publishing, 1992.

For parents and young people. Wise, insightful. Suggestions on how Jewish children — and their parents — can encounter God in their transition from dependence to emerging adulthood.

Scharlach, Bernice. "Coming of Age in Israel" in *The Hadassah Magazine Parenting Book.* Roselyn Bell, ed.; New York: Free Press, 1986, pp. 50-53.

About celebrating your child's bar/bat mitzvah in Israel. Provides information about synagogues, the *kotel* and other sites that can be used, borrowing Torahs, hotels, travel agents, guides etc.

Strassfeld, Sharon and Kathy Green. "Bar/Bat Mitzvah" in *The Jewish Family Book.* New York: Bantam Books, 1981, pp. 100-110.

Examples of how families have shaped the bar/bat mitzvah celebration to reflect their Jewish and family values. Also includes what to look for in a tutor, unique places to hold the ceremony and suggested times other than *Shabbat* morning.

"I'D LIKE TO FIND BOOKS TO HELP MY CHILDREN EXPLORE BAR/BAT MITZVAH."

Adler, Esther. *A Bar Mitzvah of a Different Kind*. New York: Jewish National Fund, 1990.

A story about an American boy's bar mitzvah in Israel.

Bush, Lawrence. *Emma Ansky-Levine and Her Mitzvah Machine*. New York: Union of American Hebrew Congregations, 1994.

Emma's "mitzvah machine" mysteriously generates motivating messages for her to begin Jewish studies toward becoming a bat mitzvah.

Elsant, Martin. *Bar Mitzvah Lessons*. Los Angeles, Calif.: Alef Design, 1993.

David's bar mitzvah fears cause him to alienate five rabbis who try to help him. Something surprising happens when he is placed in the hands of an eccentric former teacher.

Pfeffer, Susan Beth. *Turning Thirteen*. New York: Scholastic, 1988.

A pre-teen novel about an American girl approaching her bat mitzvah celebration. Humorous and sometimes tongue-in-cheek. Deals with several important contemporary Jewish issues.

Pushker, Gloria Teles. *The Belfer Bar Mitzvah*. Gretna, La.: Pelican Publishing, 1995.

A Jewish girl growing up in rural Louisiana learns about the bar mitzvah ceremony through an older cousin.

Wolff, Frieda. *Pink Slippers, Bat Mitzvah Blues*. Philadelphia: Jewish Publication Society, 1989.

A busy eighth grader struggles to understand her Jewish identity after her bat mitzvah celebration.

"*I NEED SOME BASIC BOOKS ON JEWISH PARENTING.*"

Abrams, Judith and Steven. *Jewish Parenting: Rabbinic Insights.*
   Northvale, N.J.: Jason Aronson, 1994.

Written by a rabbi/wife and pediatrician/husband team. Combines
history, medical, and personal insights for child rearing. Novel
interpretation of midrashic texts, which opens rabbinic literature to
parents searching for wisdom and guidance.

Danan, Julie Hilton. *The Jewish Parents Almanac.* Northvale, N.J.: Jason
   Aronson, 1994.

Guide for raising Jewish children from birth to the teen years.
Appropriate for families of all backgrounds. Includes fine selection of
mitzvah projects that can be done at any time, but are especially appropriate during the bar/bat mitzvah year. Chapters on "Bar/Bat Mitzvah"
and "Looking Forward to the Teen Years" are particularly relevant.

Kurshan, Neil. *Raising Your Child to be a Mensch.* New York: Ballantine,
   1989.

Stresses that the goal of parenting is to raise a kind, moral, responsible human being.

Reuben, Steven Carr. *Raising Jewish Children in a Contemporary World:
   The Modern Parent's Guide to Creating a Jewish Home.* Rocklin,
   Calif.: Prima Publishing, 1992.

Advice to parents living in an assimilated society. Gives reassurance
and nonjudgmental guidance on a practical and philosophical level.
Topics include: How to help children feel pride in their heritage,
how to celebrate Hanukah without feeling you are competing with
Christmas, and interfaith marriage.

Jewish Parenting Today, edited by Sharon Goldman and Sandy Edry.
   (Address inquiries to: *Jewish Parenting Today*, 2472 Broadway, Box
   293, New York, New York 10025; (212) 663-1864)

A monthly magazine focusing on issues affecting Jewish families in
the New York area, such as education, rituals, holidays, and popular culture.

"BAR/BAT MITZVAH HAS BROUGHT UP QUESTIONS ABOUT BEING AN INTERFAITH FAMILY."

King, Andrea. *If I'm Jewish and You're Christian, What Are the Kids?* New York: Union of American Hebrew Congregations, 1993.

Tracks the development of two composite families through the life-cycle process and compares how they manage challenges.

Dovetail, edited by Joan Hawxhurst. (Address inquiries to: Dovetail Publishing, P.O. Box 19945, Kalamazoo, MI 49019)

The only independent national periodical devoted exclusively to the challenges and opportunities of being an interfaith family.

"WE'D LIKE TO PURSUE TORAH STUDY AS A FAMILY."

Fields, Harvey J. *A Torah Commentary for Our Times.* New York: Union of American Hebrew Congregations. Vol. 1 (Genesis) and Vol. 2 (Exodus/Leviticus), 1991; Vol. 3 (Numbers/Deuteronomy), 1993.

A brief overview and modern translation of each Torah portion. In a "themes" section, particular ideas relating to the portion are developed. Opinions by commentators from different historical periods are included, as are questions for study and further discussion.

Halper, Sharon. *B'shivtecha B'veitecha, When You Sit in Your House.* Los Angeles, Calif.: Torah Aura Productions, 1994.

Weekly portions in English, followed by a question directing the family to look at the text in a variety of ways. Illustrated with cartoons to appeal to children.

Loeb, Sorel Goldberg and Barbara Binder Kadden. *Teaching Torah: A Treasury of Insights and Activities.* Denver, Colo.: Alternatives in Religious Education, Inc., 1984.

The best of teacher aids, easily adaptable for home study. Contains summaries of the portion of the week, insights and strategies, discussion questions, and activities.

A Secret Space. Produced by Roberta Hodes, 1977. Distributed by the
New York Board of Jewish Education.

A moving, sometimes humorous story of a young adolescent boy's
search for his Jewish identity. Touches upon major issues and
undercurrents in contemporary Jewish life. 78 minutes.

The Mitzvah Machine. New York: United Synagogue of America, 1988.

Basic message is that mitzvah is the norm which governs Jewish living. Good "trigger" for initiating a discussion on the meaning of
bar/bat mitzvah. Animated. 30 minutes.

The Struggle. Distributed by The Department of Education and Culture of
the World Zionist Organization, New York.

An American boy's initial reluctance to go to Israel for his bar mitzvah changes to enthusiasm as an uncle recounts his experience as a
Jewish resistance fighter for Israel's liberation. 30 minutes.

Someone Is Listening. New York: United Synagogue of America, 1985.

The story of a deaf teenager who meets a rabbi who helps prepare
him in sign language for his bar mitzvah service. 38 minutes.

The Discovery. New York: Jewish Theological Seminary.

Explores the conflicts that arise when a boy does not understand
the meaning of his forthcoming bar mitzvah ceremony. Particularly
relevant for suburban Jews in non-Orthodox congregations. 59
minutes. Comes with a study guide.

The Journey. Produced by Media Inc. and distributed by Ergo Media,
Teaneck, N.J.

A young Russian boy and an American Jewish engineer meet in
Leningrad during World War II and form a friendship that changes

both their lives. Explores the relationship between Jewish education and identity. 34 minutes.

The Good Deed. Produced and distributed by the Bureau of Jewish Education of Boston, Newton, Mass., 1992.

Depicts a bar mitzvah boy on the morning of his ceremony. Deals with such issues as parents' insensitivity to what their child is experiencing, and a child's fears and concerns. 14 minutes.

The Birthday Boy. An episode from the TV series The Wonder Years.

Kevin is jealous of Paul's upcoming bar mitzvah, which makes him wonder about his own family's traditions. Bar mitzvah as seen through the non-Jewish friend's eyes. Available from Ergo Media in Teaneck, N.J.; the Seidman Educational Resource Center at Auerbach CAJE in Melrose Park, Pa.; and the New York Board of Jewish Education.

To Jew Is Not a Verb. Produced for TV Ontario by Beacon Films, 1992.

A bar mitzvah student moves to a new city and has to find time for new friends, sports and Hebrew studies. Excellent for discussion of role conflict, self-respect, antisemitism, Jewish identity, prejudice. 15 minutes.

The Outside Chance of Maximillian Glick. South Gate Entertainment, 1988.

Story of a Jewish boy in a small town in Canada preparing simultaneously for an upcoming bar mitzvah and a piano competition. Prejudice and stereotypes are examined through a friendship with a Catholic girl and difficulties with bar mitzvah tutors. 95 minutes.

SHABBAT MORNING SERVICE OUTLINE

Cantor Marshall Portnoy

Traditionally, *Shabbat* morning service begins with brief early morning prayers called *Birkhot Hashakhar*, "Early Morning Blessings," and continues with a somewhat longer group of Psalms and prayers called *Psukey D'zimrah*, "Verses of Song." These two sections may last about half an hour. In a few Conservative congregations and in many Reform congregations, these are eliminated or severely abbreviated.

All congregations begin "formal" worship with *Sh'ma U'Virkhoteha*, "The *Sh'ma* and its blessings." This section is introduced by the "Call to Worship" known as the *Barkhu* and presents two sections of text before the *Sh'ma*. The *Sh'ma* consists of three excerpts from the Pentateuch and expresses God's oneness, our obligation to love God, to have God's precepts always in mind and to teach them to our children. It details rewards and punishments in connection with fulfilling God's commands, and reminds us of the *tallit*. Of the three excerpts, the first (Deuteronomy 6:4-10) is by far the most famous and important. The *Sh'ma* is followed by additional text. This entire section of the service concludes with the *Mi Khamokha* in which God is recalled as Israel's Redeemer.

All congregations then proceed with the *Tefillah* (often called *Amidah*), a group of seven blessings that express our link to our ancestors; God's might; God's holiness; the holiness of the Sabbath day; service to God; thanks to God; and God as our source of peace.

Following the *Tefillah* is the service for the reading of Torah. The next section of the *Shabbat* morning service is called *Musaf*, which recalls the days when an extra *Shabbat* sacrifice was made by our ancestors. It is generally not recited in Reform or Reconstructionist congregations.

All congregations end their ritual with the concluding prayers, which include the *Aleinu*, a memorial prayer called *Mourner's Kaddish*, and a closing hymn and/or benediction. In some congregations, *Kiddush*, or the blessing over wine, is also chanted.

HELPFUL HINTS FOR PARENTS OF SPECIAL NEEDS CHILDREN

Beverly Weaver

Here, the author of Chapter 21 lists guidelines for parents of children with special needs, as well as some words of advice to the children themselves.

- *Empower your child*: Bar/bat mitzvah is a major life cycle event your child's life. Remember that the event is your child's, not yours. Your child deserves a major say in different aspects of the bar/bat mitzvah celebration but must also take the major responsibility for the success of the event.
- *Find your own comfort level*: There are many options for the bar/bat mitzvah ceremony of a special needs child, but make sure that the ones you present to your child are available at your congregation and truly acceptable to you.
- *Plan, plan, plan*: It is never too early to begin thinking about bar/bat mitzvah. Time can be one of your biggest allies. But keep in mind that there is a difference between planning and obsessing. Too much pressure for too long will defeat any child, with or without special needs. It is particularly important that the house be calm for the bar/bat mitzvah boy or girl the last week before the bar/bat mitzvah ceremony. Don't leave too many errands for the last minute. This adds tension to the

household. And don't plan on any last minute learning. Repetition and relaxation are the keys.

- *Selectively share the situation*: It is important to share information about your child's learning disabilities with the key players in your child's religious education, bar/bat mitzvah planning, and bar/bat mitzvah training. However, the pre-teen and teen years can be especially difficult for special needs children, who desperately want to fit in. If your child doesn't want to share this information with everyone, respect that preference.

- *Accommodations*: There are as many ways to accommodate learning disabilities as there are disabilities. The key is to pinpoint your child's learning problems. If you can't do that yourself, there are professionals (teachers, tutors, etc.) who can help. It is well worth the time and effort. For example, two large categories of learning styles include auditory (oral) and visual (seeing or reading) learners. Since the auditory learner learns better from what he or she hears, an example of a possible learning accommodation for that student is study from a tape and oral presentations. For the visual learner, large print materials help decrease visual problems. Large print *siddurim* (prayer books) are available for purchase. Other materials may be enlarged on a photocopy machine. Computer programs which teach trope, or written materials that teach trope with color coding, are also available and may help children learn trope for the Torah and *Haftarah* readings.

  Professional tutors and teachers of special needs children who provide accommodations for secular learning are a good source of guidance to professionals in Jewish education. Seek this guidance if your congregation will not meet your needs. Your special needs child, like every other student, deserves a specialized learning plan fit exactly to his or her needs.

- *Enjoy!* Too many times we parents get so wrapped up in worry over the details of bar/bat mitzvah celebrations that we really don't enjoy them. That goes double when the child has special learning needs, and the parents are concerned about study. Remember that the congregation at a bar/bat mitzvah ceremony is the least critical audience in the world: They are already sure the bar/bat mitzvah will be wonderful, and somehow he or she always is.

HELPFUL HINTS TO A SPECIAL NEEDS CHILD

- *Believe in yourself:* You are not stupid; your learning problems are the direct result of identified learning disabilities, *not* low intelligence. You can have the bar/bat mitzvah celebration *you* want if the correct educational approach is used, and you are entitled to the necessary accommodations. Also, keep in mind that bar/bat mitzvah is not a contest. Don't measure your success against artificial markers (for example, how many pages of *Haftarah* you are chanting compared to others in your bar/bat mitzvah class). Instead, measure the success of your bar/bat mitzvah by your level of effort expended and your commitment to Judaism. These are more valid markers of success.
- *Be your own advocate:* No matter what you are studying, it can be taught in a manner appropriate for you to learn. However, not all teachers (or parents) will immediately be aware when something is being taught in a manner which doesn't make good sense to you. Don't hesitate to speak up, either to the teacher or your parents, when something does not make sense. There is nothing wrong in saying "I don't understand when you talk fast" or "It is too confusing when we study so much in one

day." People do not look down on you for advocating for yourself. They respect you for it.

- *Enjoy!* Bar/bat mitzvah happens only one time in your whole life. It is natural to be nervous, but don't let worry get out of hand and ruin your time. Especially keep in mind that those in the congregation on the day of your bar/bat mitzvah ceremony already know you are wonderful!

SELECTED BIBLIOGRAPHY

RECOMMENDED SOURCES FOR ENGLISH READINGS DURING THE BAR/BAT MITZVAH SERVICE

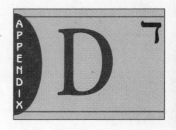

Cantor Helen Leneman

T he following books contain appropriate and meaningful readings which can be used in your personalized service booklet.

Gates of Prayer. New York: Central Conference of American Rabbis, 1975;

Gates of Repentance. New York: Central Conference of American Rabbis, 1984. Each of these Reform prayerbooks has a "Meditations and Readings" section.

Siddur Sim Shalom. New York: The Rabbinical Assembly, United Synagogue of America, 1985. This Conservative prayerbook has sections entitled "Readings on Various Themes" and "Reflections."

Kol Haneshamah. Wyncote, Pa.: The Reconstructionist Press, 1994. The new Reconstructionist prayerbook has a "Readings" section. In addition, interpretations and readings can be found throughout the book.

The Judaic Tradition: Jewish Writings from Antiquity to the Modern Age. Selected and translated by Nahum N. Glazer. Northvale, N.J.: Jason Aronson Inc., 1987. A large and varied collection of readings from the Jewish tradition.

GLOSSARY

Aliyah (plural, *aliyot*)
Literally, "going up." The ascent to the *bimah* to say the blessings over the Torah scroll.

Amidah
Literally, the "standing" prayer. The nineteen prayers (seven on *Shabbat* and festivals) that constitute the main body of Jewish liturgy; also known as *tefillah* and the *shemoneh esrei.*

Bimah
The raised platform or pulpit in most synagogues where the service is conducted.

Chumash (from *chameish*, "five")
The Pentateuch (Five Books of Moses), or a book containing the Pentateuch.

Haftarah
Literally, "completion." The reading of the section from the Prophets for a particular *Shabbat.*

Halachah
Jewish law.

Havdalah
Literally, "separation," "distinction." The ceremony that ends *Shabbat.*

Havurah (plural, *havurot*)
An independent, participant-led Jewish fellowship group; or, a semi-independent study or prayer group within a synagogue.

Hazzan
The cantor, also known as the *shaliach tzibur*, the community prayer leader.

Kashrut
The Jewish dietary laws.

Kiddush
The prayer accompanied by wine or grape juice and recited before dinner on the eve of the Sabbath or a festival, to inaugurate the day and proclaim its sanctity; also, the food and wine that is customarily served in the synagogue after morning services on the Sabbath or festival.

Kosher
Food that may be eaten, according to the Jewish dietary laws.

Maariv
Evening prayer service.

Mincha
Afternoon prayer service.

Mitzvah (plural, mitzvot)
An obligation of Jewish life.

Musaf
The "additional" prayer in traditional liturgy. Recalls the ancient sacrificial rites of the Temple (the *musaf* or additional sacrifices) and repeats some themes covered earlier in the liturgy.

Parasha

The Torah portion of the week. Also sometimes referred to as the *sedra*.

Shabbat

The sabbath.

Sh'ma

A central prayer of the worship service. Essentially a statement of faith which is derived from Deuteronomy, Chapter 6: "Hear O Israel, the Lord is our God, the Lord is One."

Shul

The Yiddish word for "synagogue."

Simcha

"A joyous event." Often used to refer to a bar or bat mitzvah ceremony, or other celebrations.

Tallit

A prayer shawl.

Tefillah

The major section of Jewish liturgy, also known as the *Amidah* (standing prayer). The generic term for Jewish worship.

Torah

Literally, "teaching" or "direction." Narrowly, the first part of the Hebrew Bible that is read from the scroll; broadly, all Jewish sacred literature and by implication, all of Judaism.

Tzedakah

The *mitzvah* of sacred giving.

Yad

The thin pointer shaped at the end like a hand, which a reader of Torah uses so as not to lose his/her place.

ABOUT THE CONTRIBUTORS

Helen Leneman, the editor of this book and a contributor to it, specializes in bar/bat mitzvah education. She has worked as a cantor and a b'nai mitzvah teacher in Los Angeles and Baltimore and chairs the B'nai Mitzvah Educators Network of CAJE (the Coalition for the Advancement of Jewish Education). The Network has over 300 members in the U.S. and abroad. She has a B.A. from UCLA and an M.A. in Judaic Studies from Hebrew Union College-Jewish Institute of Religion in Los Angeles, and studied cantorial liturgy with cantors Allan Michelson (z"l) and William Sharlin. She is the author of *Bar/Bat Mitzvah Education: A Sourcebook*. She is an Associate member of the American Conference of Cantors, and a member of the American Academy of Religion and Society of Biblical Literature. Cantor Leneman directs an outreach program for unaffiliated families who wish to celebrate their children's becoming bar or bat mitzvah. She lives with her family in Rockville, Maryland; their daughter became bat mitzvah in 1992.

Aaron Bergman is the rabbi of Congregation Beth Abraham Hillel Moses in West Bloomfield, Michigan and former rabbi-in-residence of the Hillel Day School of Detroit. He is a graduate of the University of Michigan and The Jewish Theological Seminary. Rabbi Bergman lives with his wife Ruth and their two daughters in West Bloomfield. In his spare time, Rabbi Bergman paints and plays blues guitar.

Dr. Judith Davis is a licensed family therapist who practices in Amherst, Massachusetts and teaches at the University of Massachusetts in Amherst. She has published several articles on the bar/bat mitzvah ceremony as a family's rite of passage. Her book, *Mazel Tov: Mining the Magic of Your Child's Bar/Bat Mitzvah: A Family Therapist Talks to Parents*, explores the psychological and developmental opportunities inherent in the bar/bat mitzvah process.

Neal Gendler is a reporter at the Minneapolis Tribune. He has taught journalism at the University of Wisconsin-River Falls and the University of Minnesota. He began working in Twin Cities radio in the 1960s and later became an announcer/technician at the area's only full-time classical music FM station.

Donna R. Hart holds a B.A. in Psychology, an M.A. in Early Childhood Education, and a Ph.D. in Education and Human Development. Dr. Hart has worked as an educator since 1970, with a focus on children with special needs. She works with Washington D.C. and Maryland public school systems in training and staff development and has designed and taught courses at local universities.

Joan C. Hawxhurst is the editor of *Dovetail: A Newsletter By and For Jewish/Christian Families*, the only independent national periodical devoted exclusively to the challenges and opportunities of life in an interfaith family. A Methodist, Hawxhurst lives with her Jewish husband and daughter in Kalamazoo, Michigan.

Missy Cohen Lavintman, education director at B'nai Emet Synagogue in St. Louis Park, Minnesota, has a B.A. in Hebrew education and an M.A. in education. She has taught at synagogue and community schools and at the University of Minnesota. Since 1975, she has taught at the Talmud Torah of

Minneapolis. Lavintman lives in Golden Valley, Minnesota, with her husband and five children.

Nechama Liss-Levinson, Ph.D. is a psychologist and psychoanalyst in private practice. The author of many articles on developmental milestones in the Jewish family, she has also written *When a Grandparent Dies: A Kid's Own Remembering Workbook for Dealing with Shiva and the Year Beyond* (Jewish Lights Publishing, Woodstock, Vt.). She lives on Long Island, New York with her husband and two daughters.

Marshall Portnoy is the hazzan of Main Line Reform Temple in Wynnewood, Pennsylvania. A graduate of Yale University and The Jewish Theological Seminary, he has written two books on Jewish music. Cantor Portnoy and his wife, Dr. Jane Portnoy, live outside Philadelphia with their two children.

Lena Romanoff has a B.S. in nursing and an M.A. in educational psychology. She is the founder and chair of the Jewish Converts and Interfaith Network of the Coalition for the Advancement of Jewish Education (CAJE). She wrote *Your People, My People — Finding Acceptance and Fulfillment as a Jew by Choice* and directed and produced the educational video, "*Who Am I?*", which deals with intermarriage and religious identity from the child's perspective. Romanoff counsels, organizes conferences and workshops, and lectures widely on conversion, intermarriage and inter-dating. She underwent Orthodox conversion in 1973 and lives in Penn Valley with her husband and two sons.

Jeffrey K. Salkin is rabbi of Central Synagogue of Nassau County in Rockville Centre, New York. He earned a Doctor of Ministry degree at Princeton Theological Seminary, has taught rabbinic literature at Hebrew Union College – Jewish Institute of Religion, and teaches in Hebrew Union College's Doctor of Ministry program.

He has written numerous articles, as well as *Putting God on the Guest List: How to Reclaim the Spiritual Meaning of Your Child's Bar or Bat Mitzvah* and *Being God's Partner: How to Find the Hidden Link between Spirituality and Your Work* (both Jewish Lights Publishing, Woodstock, Vt.). He is married to Nina Rubin Salkin. Their son, Samuel, will probably become bar mitzvah on the last Labor Day weekend of the century.

Sandy Eisenberg Sasso is rabbi of Congregation Beth-El Zedeck of Indianapolis. A teacher and storyteller, she has led many workshops on teaching youngsters about God. The author of *God's Paintbrush, In God's Name* and *But God Remembered: Stories of Women from Creation to the Promised Land* (all Jewish Lights Publishing, Woodstock, Vt.), Rabbi Sasso is also past president of the Reconstructionist Rabbinical Association. She was the second woman ever to be ordained a rabbi (in 1974), and the first rabbi to become a mother. She and her husband, Dennis, were the first practicing rabbinical couple in world history.

Susan B. Stone was ordained at the Hebrew Union College – Jewish Institute of Religion in 1983. Spiritual leader of Temple Beth Shalom in Hudson, Ohio, Rabbi Stone looks forward to her sons, Charlie and Jake, becoming b'nai mitzvah.

Susie Tatarka was born in the Philippines and grew up in Israel. She has degrees in literature and linguistics from Tel Aviv University and has worked in Jewish education in the Twin Cities since 1970. Ms. Tatarka is the education director for the Adath Jeshurun Congregation of Minneapolis.

Barbara Wachs holds a Ph.D. from The Jewish Theological Seminary. The Consultant for Family and Adolescence at the Auerbach Central Agency for Jewish Education in Greater Philadelphia and a visiting instructor at Gratz College, she is also the chair of the Family Education Network of the Coalition for the Advancement of Jewish Education.

Beverly Weaver has worked professionally with special needs children since 1991. She teaches at Gesher Jewish Day School in Alexandria, Virginia, and tutors at Washington D.C.'s Kingsbury Center, which offers comprehensive services for children and adults with special learning needs. Weaver lives in Alexandria, Virginia with her husband, Don, and their three sons.

Sally Weber, a licensed clinical social worker, is the Regional Director of Jewish Family Service of Los Angeles, Adult and Children's Services for the San Fernando Valley. She is a faculty member of the Whizin Center on the Jewish Family at the University of Judaism and a lecturer at the Graduate School of Jewish Communal service at Hebrew Union College – Jewish Institute of Religion. She has written many articles on the changing Jewish family and is co-author of *Shalom Bayit: A Jewish Response to Child Abuse and Domestic Violence.*

NOTES

NOTES

About JEWISH LIGHTS Publishing

People of all faiths and backgrounds yearn for books that attract, engage, educate and spiritually inspire.

Our principal goal is to stimulate thought and help all people learn about who the Jewish People are, where they come from, and what the future can be made to hold. While people of our diverse Jewish heritage are the primary audience, our books speak to people in the Christian world as well and will broaden their understanding of Judaism and the roots of their own faith.

We bring to you authors who are at the forefront of spiritual thought and experience. While each has something different to say, they all say it in a voice that you can hear.

Our books are designed to welcome you and then to engage, stimulate and inspire. We judge our success not only by whether or not our books are beautiful and commercially successful, but by whether or not they make a difference in your life.

We at Jewish Lights take great care to produce beautiful books that present meaningful spiritual content in a form that reflects the art of making high quality books. Therefore, we want to acknowledge those who contributed to the production of this book.

PRODUCTION
Maria O'Donnell

EDITORIAL & PROOFREADING
Sandra Korinchak

BOOK DESIGN
Reuben Kantor, Allston, Massachusetts

COVER DESIGN
Donna Wohlfarth, Keene, New Hampshire

TYPE
Set in ITC Benguiat Gothic and Sabon
Reuben Kantor, Allston, Massachusetts

COVER PRINTING
Phoenix Color Corp., Hingham, Massachusetts

PRINTING AND BINDING
Royal Book, Norwich, Connecticut

THE FEDERATION OF JEWISH MEN'S CLUBS

Art of Jewish Living Series

THE SHABBAT SEDER
by Dr. Ron Wolfson

The Shabbat Seder is a concise step-by-step guide designed to teach people the meaning and importance of this weekly celebration, as well as its practices. The activities of the Friday evening ritual are set out in a straightforward, simple way, along with instructions on how to perform them, and the information is presented through an exploration of the Shabbat ceremonies of real families representing a cross section of modern Jewish life.

Each chapter corresponds to one of ten steps which together comprise the Shabbat dinner ritual, and looks at the *concepts*, *objects*, and *meanings* behind the specific activity or ritual act. *The Shabbat Seder* is designed in a unique, easy-to-read format for people with varying degrees of Hebrew skills; the blessings that accompany the meal are written in both Hebrew and English, and accompanied by English transliteration. Also included are a question and answer section and a "Shabbat Gallery" offering craft projects, recipes, discussion ideas and other creative suggestions for enriching the Shabbat experience.

"A how-to book in the best sense...."

—Dr. David Lieber, President, University of Judaism, Los Angeles

7 x 9, 272 pp. Quality Paperback, ISBN 1-879045-90-7 **$14.95**

Also available are these helpful companions to *The Shabbat Seder*:	
•Booklet of the Blessings and Songs	ISBN 1-879045-91-5 $4.00
•Audiocassette of the Blessings	DNO3 $4.00
•Teacher's Guide	ISBN 1-879045-92-3 $4.95

A TIME TO MOURN,
A TIME TO COMFORT
A Guide to Jewish Bereavement and Comfort
by Dr. Ron Wolfson

A guide to meeting the needs of those who mourn and those who seek to provide comfort in times of sadness. While this book is written from a layperson's point of view, it also includes the specifics for funeral preparations and practical guidance for preparing the home and family to sit *shiva*. Advice is given for attending a Jewish funeral, how to help during *shiva*, what to say to the mourners, and what to write in a condolence letter. Special sections deal with specific situations of modern life, including deaths from AIDS, helping young children grieve and understand *shiva*, and mourning the death of an infant or child.

"A sensitive and perceptive guide to Jewish tradition. Both those who mourn and those who comfort will find it a map to accompany them through the whirlwind."

—Deborah E. Lipstadt, Emory University

"Speaks in many voices: the voices of those who have endured grief, the voices of rabbis who deal daily with tragedy, the voices of those who are spiritually searching, and the voices of those who have found their own path through dark times."

—Dr. David J. Wolpe, author of
Healer of Shattered Hearts

7 x 9, 320 pp. Quality Paperback, ISBN 1-879045-96-6 **$16.95**

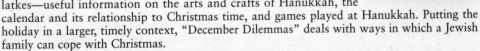

Bring Spirituality into Your Daily Life

BEING GOD'S PARTNER
How to Find the Hidden Link Between Spirituality and Your Work

by *Jeffrey K. Salkin* Introduction by *Norman Lear*

A book that will challenge people of every denomination to reconcile the cares of work and soul. A groundbreaking book about spirituality and the work world, from a Jewish perspective. Helps the reader find God in the ethical striving and search for meaning in the professions and in business. Looks at our modern culture of workaholism and careerism, and offers practical suggestions for balancing your professional life and spiritual self.

Being God's Partner will inspire people of all faiths and no faith to find greater meaning in their work, and see themselves doing God's work in the world.

"His is an eloquent voice, bearing an important and concrete message of authentic Jewish religion. The book is engaging, easy to read and hard to put down — and it will make a difference and change people."

> — Jacob Neusner, Distinguished Research Professor of Religious Studies, University of South Florida, author of *The Doubleday Anchor Reference Library Introduction to Rabbinic Literature*

6" x 9", 192 pp. Hardcover, ISBN 1-879045-37-0 **$19.95**

SELF, STRUGGLE & CHANGE
Family Conflict Stories in Genesis and Their Healing Insights for Our Lives

by *Norman J. Cohen*

How do I find greater wholeness in my life and in my family's life?

The stress of late-20th-century living only brings new variations to timeless personal struggles. The people described by the biblical writers of Genesis were in situations and relationships very much like our own. We identify with them. Their stories still speak to us because they are about the same problems we deal with every day. A modern master of biblical interpretation brings us greater understanding of the ancient text and of ourselves in this intriguing re-telling of conflict between husband and wife, father and son, brothers, and sisters.

"Cohen's commentaries cut to the quick—his Torah is alive and we are the protagonists....The midrash he teaches us is therapeutic, it results in our growth."

> —Rabbi Burton L. Vistozky, JTS

6" x 9", 224 pp. Hardcover, ISBN 1-879045-19-2 **$21.95**

SO THAT YOUR VALUES LIVE ON
Ethical Wills & How To Prepare Them

Edited by *Rabbi Jack Riemer & Professor Nathaniel Stampfer*

A cherished Jewish tradition, ethical wills—parents writing to children or grandparents to grandchildren—sum up what people have learned and express what they want most for, and from, their loved ones. Includes an intensive guide, "How to Write Your Own Ethical Will," and a topical index. A marvelous treasury of wills: Herzl, Sholom Aleichem, Israelis, Holocaust victims, contemporary American Jews.

"This remarkable volume will enrich all those who will read it and meditate upon its infinite wisdom." — *Elie Wiesel*

6"x 9", 272 pp. Quality Paperback, ISBN 1-879045-34-6 **$16.95**

Add Greater Meaning to Your Life

Add Greater Understanding to Your Life

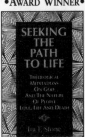

Motivation & Inspiration for Recovery

TWELVE JEWISH STEPS TO RECOVERY
A Personal Guide To Turning From Alcoholism & Other Addictions...Drugs, Food, Gambling, Sex

by *Rabbi Kerry M. Olitzky* & *Stuart A. Copans, M.D.*
Preface by Abraham J. Twerski, M.D.
Introduction by Rabbi Sheldon Zimmerman
Illustrations by Maty Grünberg
"Getting Help" by JACS Foundation

A Jewish perspective on the Twelve Steps of addiction recovery programs with consolation, inspiration and motivation for recovery. It draws from traditional sources, and quotes from what recovering Jewish people say about their experiences with addictions of all kinds. Inspiring illustrations of the twelve gates of the Old City of Jerusalem.

Experts Praise *Twelve Jewish Steps to Recovery*

"Recommended reading for people of all denominations." — Rabbi Abraham J. Twerski, M.D.

"I read Twelve Jewish Steps with the eyes of a Christian and came away renewed in my heart. I felt like I had visited my Jewish roots. These authors have deep knowledge of recovery as viewed by Alcoholics Anonymous." — Rock J. Stack, M.A., L.L.D. Manager of Clinical/Pastoral Education, Hazelden Foundation

"This book is the first aimed directly at helping the addicted person and family. Everyone affected or interested should read it." — Sheila B. Blume, M.D., C.A.C., Medical Director, Alcoholism, Chemical Dependency and Compulsive Gambling Programs, South Oaks Hospital, Amityville, NY

Readers Praise *Twelve Jewish Steps to Recovery*

"A God-send. Literally. A book from the higher power." — New York, NY

"Looking forward to using it in my practice." —Michigan City, IN

"Made me feel as though Twelve Steps were for me, too." — Long Beach, CA

"Excellent—changed my life." — Elkhart Lake, WI

6" x 9", 136 pp. Quality Paperback, ISBN 1-879045-09-5 **$13.95**   HC, ISBN -08-7 **$19.95**

RECOVERY FROM *Codependence* Jewish Twelve Steps Guide to Healing Your Soul

by *Rabbi Kerry M. Olitzky*
Foreword by *Marc Galanter, M.D., Director, Division of Alcoholism & Drug Abuse, NYU Medical Center*
Afterword by *Harriet Rossetto, Director, Gateways Beit T'shuvah*

For the estimated 90% of America struggling with the addiction of a family member or loved one, or involved in a dysfunctional family or relationship. A follow-up to the groundbreaking *Twelve Jewish Steps to Recovery*.

"The disease of chemical dependency is also a family illness. Rabbi Olitzky offers spiritual hope and support." —*Jerry Spicer, President, Hazelden*

"Another major step forward in finding the sources and resources of healing, both physical and spiritual, in our tradition." —*Rabbi Sheldon Zimmerman, Temple Emanu-El, Dallas, TX*

6" x 9", 160 pp. Quality Paperback Original, ISBN 1-879045-32-X **$13.95**   HC, ISBN -27-3 **$21.95**

Motivation & Inspiration for Recovery

RENEWED EACH DAY

Daily Twelve Step Recovery Meditations Based on the Bible

by *Rabbi Kerry M. Olitzky* & *Aaron Z.*

VOLUME I: Genesis & Exodus
Introduction by *Rabbi Michael A. Signer*
Afterword by JACS Foundation

VOLUME II: Leviticus, Numbers & Deuteronomy
Introduction by *Sharon M. Strassfeld*
Afterword by *Rabbi Harold M. Schulweis*

Using a seven day/weekly guide format, a recovering person and a spiritual leader who is reaching out to addicted people reflect on the traditional weekly Bible reading. They bring strong spiritual support for daily living and recovery from addictions of all kinds: alcohol, drugs, eating, gambling and sex. A profound sense of the religious spirit soars through their words and brings all people in Twelve Step recovery programs home to a rich and spiritually enlightening tradition.

"Meets a vital need; it offers a chance for people turning from alcoholism and addiction to renew their spirits and draw upon the Jewish tradition to guide and enrich their lives."
—*Rabbi Irving (Yitz) Greenberg, President, CLAL,*
The National Jewish Center for Learning and Leadership

"Will benefit anyone familiar with a 'religion of the Book.' Jews, Christians, Muslims. . . ."
—*Ernest Kurtz, author of* Not God: A History of Alcoholics
Anonymous & The Spirituality of Imperfection

"An enduring impact upon the faith community as it seeks to blend the wisdom of the ages represented in the tradition with the twelve steps to recovery and wholeness."
—*Robert H. Albers, Ph.D., Editor,* Journal of Ministry in Addiction & Recovery

Beautiful Two-Volume Slipcased Set

6"x 9", V. I, 224 pp. / V. II, 280 pp., Quality Paperback Original,
ISBN 1-879045-21-4 **$27.90**

ONE HUNDRED BLESSINGS EVERY DAY

Daily Twelve Step Recovery Affirmations, Exercises for Personal Growth & Renewal Reflecting Seasons of the Jewish Year

by *Dr. Kerry M. Olitzky*
with selected meditations prepared by *Rabbi James Stone Goodman,*
Danny Siegel, and *Rabbi Gordon Tucker*
Foreword by *Rabbi Neil Gillman,*
The Jewish Theological Seminary of America
Afterword by *Dr. Jay Holder, Director, Exodus Treatment Center*

Recovery is a conscious choice from moment to moment, day in and day out. In this helpful and healing book of daily recovery meditations, Rabbi Olitzky gives us words to live by day after day, throughout the annual cycle of holiday observances and special Sabbaths of the Jewish calendar.

For those facing the struggles of daily living, *One Hundred Blessings Every Day* brings solace and hope to anyone who is open to healing and to the recovery-oriented teachings that can be gleaned from the Bible and Jewish tradition.

4¹/2" x 6¹/2", 432 pp., Quality Paperback Original, ISBN 1-879045-30-3 **$14.95**

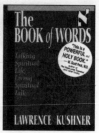

Spiritual Inspiration for Family Life

THE *NEW* JEWISH BABY BOOK
Names, Ceremonies, Customs — A Guide for Today's Families

by *Anita Diamant*
Foreword by *Rabbi Norman J. Cohen, Dean, HUC–JIR, NYC*
Introduction by *Rabbi Amy Eilberg*

A complete guide to the customs and rituals for welcoming a new child to the world and into the Jewish community, and for commemorating this joyous event in family life–whatever your family constellation. Updated, revised and expanded edition of the highly acclaimed *The Jewish Baby Book*. Includes new ceremonies for girls, celebrations in interfaith families. Also contains a unique directory of names that reflects the rich diversity of the Jewish experience.

"A book that all Jewish parents—no matter how religious—will find fascinating as well as useful. It is a perfect shower or new baby gift." — Pamela Abrams, Exec. Editor, *Parents Magazine*

6"x 9", 328 pp. Quality Paperback Original, ISBN 1-879045-28-1 **$15.95**

PUTTING GOD ON THE GUEST LIST •AWARD WINNER•
How to Reclaim the Spiritual Meaning of Your Child's Bar or Bat Mitzvah

"Best Religion Book of the Year"

by *Rabbi Jeffrey K. Salkin*
Foreword by *Rabbi Sandy Eisenberg Sasso*
Introduction by *Rabbi William H. Lebeau, Vice Chancellor, JTS*

Joining explanation, instruction and inspiration, helps parent and child truly *be there* when the moment of Sinai is recreated in their lives. Asks and answers such fundamental questions as how did Bar and Bat Mitzvah originate? What is the lasting significance of the event? How to make the event more spiritually meaningful?

"Shows the way to restore spirituality and depth to every young Jew's most important rite of passage."
— Rabbi Joseph Telushkin, author of *Jewish Literacy*

6"x 9", 184 pp. Quality Paperback, ISBN 1-879045-10-9 **$14.95** HC, ISBN -20-6 **$21.95**

BAR/BAT MITZVAH BASICS
A Practical Family Guide to Coming of Age Together

NEW!

Edited by Cantor Helen Leneman
Foreword by Rabbi Jeffrey K. Salkin
Preface by Rabbi Julie Gordon

For the first time in one book, all who are directly involved in bar and bat mitzvah offer their practical insights into how the process can be made easier and more enjoyable for the whole family.

6" x 9", 240 pp. Quality Paperback, ISBN 1-879045-54-0 **$16.95** HC -51-6 **$24.95**

EMBRACING THE COVENANT
Converts to Judaism Talk About Why & How

Edited and with Introductions by Rabbi Allan Berkowitz & Patti Moskovitz

A companion to the conversion process for Jews-by-Choice and their families. Through personal experiences of converts to Judaism, and information on the process itself, illuminates this most pivotal of life-decisions.

6" x 9", 184 pp. (est) Quality Paperback, ISBN 1-879045-50-8 **$15.95**

Embracing the Covenant

Converts to Judaism Talk About Why & How

Edited and with introductions by Rabbi Allan Berkowitz & Patti Moskovitz

NEW!

Spiritual Inspiration for Family Life

MOURNING & MITZVAH
A Guided Journal for Walking the Mourner's Path
Through Grief to Healing • WITH OVER 60 GUIDED EXERCISES •

by *Anne Brener, L.C.S.W.*
Foreword by *Rabbi Jack Riemer*
Introduction by *Rabbi William Cutter*

"Fully engaging in mourning means you will be a different person than before you began."

For those who mourn a death, for those who would help them, for those who face a loss of any kind, Anne Brener teaches us the power and strength available to us in the fully experienced mourning process. Guided writing exercises help stimulate the processes of both conscious and unconscious healing.

"A stunning book! It offers an exploration in depth of the place where psychology and religious ritual intersect, and the name of that place is Truth."
　　　　—Rabbi Harold Kushner, author of *When Bad Things Happen to Good People*
"This book is marvelous. It is a work that I wish I had written. It is the best book on this subject that I have ever seen."
　　　　—Rabbi Levi Meier, Ph.D., *Chaplain, Cedars Sinai Medical Center, Los Angeles, Orthodox Rabbi, Clinical Psychologist*

7 1/2" x 9", 288 pp. Quality Paperback Original, ISBN 1-879045-23-0 **$19.95**

NEW!　　WHEN A GRANDPARENT DIES
A Kid's Own Remembering Workbook for
Dealing with Shiva and the Year Beyond
by *Nechama Liss-Levinson, Ph.D.*

The death of a grandparent is often a child's first encounter with grief. Drawing insights from both psychology and Jewish tradition, this workbook helps children participate in the process of mourning, offering guided exercises, rituals, and places to write, draw, list, create, and express their feelings.

"Will bring support, guidance, and understanding for countless children, teachers, and health professionals."
　　　　—Rabbi Earl A. Grollman, D.D., author of *Talking about Death*

8" x 10", 48 pp. Hardcover, illus., 2-color text, ISBN 1-879045-44-3 **$14.95**

HEALING OF SOUL, HEALING OF BODY
Spiritual Leaders Unfold the Strength and Solace in Psalms

Edited by *Rabbi Simkha Y. Weintraub, CSW*
A Project of The Jewish Healing Center

A source of solace for those who are facing illness, as well as those who care for them. Ten Psalms newly translated, making them clear and accessible, and each one introduced by an eminent rabbi, men and women reflecting different movements and backgrounds. To all who are living with the pain and uncertainty of illness, this spiritual resource offers an anchor of spiritual comfort.

"This gentle book is a luminous gem of wisdom."
　　　　—Larry Dossey, M.D., author of *Healing Words: The Power of Prayer & the Practice of Medicine*

6" x 9", 128 pp. Quality Paperback Original, illus., 2-color text, ISBN 1-879045-31-1 **$14.95**

Coming Summer '96: Finding Joy:
A Practical Spiritual Guide to Happiness
by Dannel Schwartz with Mark Hass. 6 x 9, 192 pp (est), HC, ISBN 1-879045-53-2 **$19.95**

Children's

BUT GOD REMEMBERED
Stories of Women from Creation to the Promised Land
by *Sandy Eisenberg Sasso*

Full color illustrations by *Bethanne Andersen*

NON-SECTARIAN, NON-DENOMINATIONAL.
A fascinating collection of four different stories of women only briefly mentioned in biblical tradition and religious texts, but never before explored. Award-winning author Sasso brings to life the intriguing stories of Lilith, Serach, Bityah, and the Daughters of Z, courageous and strong women from ancient tradition. All teach important values through their faith and actions.

For ages 8 and up

"Exquisite....a book of beauty, strength and spirituality."
—Association of Bible Teachers

9" x 12", 32 pp. Hardcover, Full color illus., ISBN 1-879045-43-5 **$16.95**

IN GOD'S NAME
For ages 4-8

by *Sandy Eisenberg Sasso*
Full color illustrations by *Phoebe Stone*

MULTICULTURAL, NON-SECTARIAN, NON-DENOMINATIONAL.
Like an ancient myth in its poetic text and vibrant illustrations, this modern fable about the search for God's name celebrates the diversity and, at the same time, the unity of all the people of the world. Each seeker claims he or she alone knows the answer. Finally, they come together and learn what God's name really is, sharing the ultimate harmony of belief in one God by people of all faiths, all backgrounds.

• AWARD WINNER •

"I got goose bumps when I read *In God's Name*, its language and illustrations are that moving. This is a book children will love and the whole family will cherish for its beauty and power."
—Francine Klagsbrun, author of *Mixed Feelings: Love, Hate, Rivalry, and Reconciliation among Brothers and Sisters*

"What a lovely, healing book!"
—Madeleine L'Engle

9" x 12", 32 pp. Hardcover, Full color illus., ISBN 1-879045-26-5 **$16.95**

> **Selected by Parent Council Ltd.™**

For children K-4

GOD'S PAINTBRUSH
by *Sandy Eisenberg Sasso*
Full color illustrations by *Annette Compton*

MULTICULTURAL, NON-SECTARIAN, NON-DENOMINATIONAL.
Invites children of all faiths and backgrounds to encounter God openly in their own lives. Wonderfully interactive, provides questions adult and child can explore together at the end of each episode.

"An excellent way to honor the imaginative breadth and depth of the spiritual life of the young."
—Dr. Robert Coles, Harvard University

• AWARD WINNER •

11"x 8½", 32 pp. Hardcover, Full color illustrations, ISBN 1-879045-22-2 **$16.95**

THE 11TH COMMANDMENT
Wisdom from Our Children
by The Children of America

MULTICULTURAL, NON-SECTARIAN, NON-DENOMINATIONAL.

"If there were an Eleventh Commandment, what would it be?"
Children of many religious denominations across America answer this question—in their own drawings and words—in *The 11th Commandment*. This full-color collection of "Eleventh Commandments" reveals kids' ideas about how people should respond to God.

8" x 10", 48 pp. Hardcover, Full color illustrations, ISBN 1-879045-46-X **$16.95**

# of Copies	Order Information	$ Amount

_____	Aspects of Rabbinic Theology (pb), $18.95
_____	Bar/Bat Mitzvah Basics (hc), $24.95; (pb), $16.95
_____	Being God's Partner (hc), $19.95
_____	But God Remembered (hc), $16.95
_____	The Earth Is the Lord's (pb), $12.95
_____	The 11th Commandment (hc), $16.95
_____	Embracing the Covenant (pb), $15.95
_____	The Empty Chair (hc), $9.95
_____	Finding Joy (hc), $19.95
_____	God & the Big Bang (hc), $21.95
_____	God's Paintbrush (hc), $16.95
_____	Godwrestling—Round 2 (hc), $23.95
_____	Hanukkah (pb), $14.95
_____	Healing of Soul, Healing of Body (pb), $14.95
_____	How to Be a Perfect Stranger (hc), $24.95
_____	In God's Name (hc), $16.95
_____	The Last Trial (pb), $17.95
_____	Lifecycles, Volume 1 (hc), $24.95
_____	Lifecycles, Volume 2 (hc), $24.95
_____	Mourning & Mitzvah (pb), $19.95
_____	The NEW Jewish Baby Book (pb), $15.95
_____	One Hundred Blessings Every Day, (pb), $14.95
_____	A Passion for Truth (pb), $18.95
_____	Passover Seder (pb), $14.95
_____	Putting God on the Guest List (hc), $21.95; (pb), $14.95
_____	Recovery From Codependence, (hc) $21.95; (pb) $13.95
_____	Renewed Each Day, 2-Volume Set, (pb) $27.90
_____	Seeking the Path to Life (pb), $14.95
_____	Self, Struggle & Change (hc), $21.95
_____	Shabbat Seder (pb), $14.95
_____	So That Your Values Live On (hc), $23.95; (pb), $16.95
_____	Spirit of Renewal (hc), $22.95; (pb), $16.95
_____	A Time to Mourn (pb), $16.95
_____	Tormented Master (pb), $17.95
_____	Twelve Jewish Steps To Recovery, (hc) $19.95; (pb) $13.95
_____	When a Grandparent Dies (hc), $14.95
_____	Your Word Is Fire (pb), $14.95
_____	Other:_____

• The Kushner Series •

_____	The Book of Letters Popular Hardcover Edition (hc), $24.95
_____	The Book of Words (hc), $21.95
_____	God Was in This Place... (hc) $21.95; (pb) $16.95
_____	Honey from the Rock (pb), $14.95
_____	Invisible Lines of Connection (hc), $21.95
_____	River of Light (pb), $14.95

For s/h, add $3.50 for the first book, $2.00 each add'l book (to a max. of $12.00) $ s/h

TOTAL _____

Check enclosed for $ _____ *payable to:* JEWISH LIGHTS Publishing

Charge my credit card: ☐ MasterCard   ☐ Visa   ☐ AMEX

Credit Card # _____ Expires _____

Name on card _____

Signature _____ Phone (_____) _____

Name _____

Street _____

City / State / Zip _____

Phone, fax, or mail to: JEWISH LIGHTS Publishing

P. O. Box 237, Sunset Farm Offices, Route 4, Woodstock, Vermont 05091

Tel (802) 457-4000   *Fax* (802) 457-4004

Credit card orders (800) 962-4544 (9AM–5PM ET Monday–Friday)

Generous discounts on quantity orders. SATISFACTION GUARANTEED. Prices subject to change.

AVAILABLE FROM BETTER BOOKSTORES.
TRY YOUR BOOKSTORE FIRST.

_____ Aspects of Rabbinic Theology (pb), $18.95   _____

_____ Bar/Bat Mitzvah Basics (hc), $24.95; (pb), $16.95   _____

_____ Being God's Partner (hc), $19.95   _____

_____ But God Remembered (hc), $16.95   _____

_____ The Earth Is the Lord's (pb), $12.95   _____

_____ The 11th Commandment (hc), $16.95   _____

_____ Embracing the Covenant (pb), $15.95   _____

_____ The Empty Chair (hc), $9.95   _____

_____ Finding Joy (hc), $19.95   _____

_____ God & the Big Bang (hc), $21.95   _____

_____ God's Paintbrush (hc), $16.95   _____

_____ Godwrestling—Round 2 (hc), $23.95   _____

_____ Hanukkah (pb), $14.95   _____

_____ Healing of Soul, Healing of Body (pb), $14.95   _____

_____ How to Be a Perfect Stranger (hc), $24.95   _____

_____ In God's Name (hc), $16.95   _____

_____ The Last Trial (pb), $17.95   _____

_____ Lifecycles, Volume 1 (hc), $24.95   _____

_____ Lifecycles, Volume 2 (hc), $24.95   _____

_____ Mourning & Mitzvah (pb), $19.95   _____

_____ The NEW Jewish Baby Book (pb), $15.95   _____

_____ One Hundred Blessings Every Day, (pb), $14.95   _____

_____ A Passion for Truth (pb), $18.95   _____

_____ Passover Seder (pb), $14.95   _____

_____ Putting God on the Guest List (hc), $21.95; (pb), $14.95   _____

_____ Recovery From Codependence, (hc) $21.95; (pb) $13.95   _____

_____ Renewed Each Day, 2-Volume Set, (pb) $27.90   _____

_____ Seeking the Path to Life (pb), $14.95   _____

_____ Self, Struggle & Change (hc), $21.95   _____

_____ Shabbat Seder (pb), $14.95   _____

_____ So That Your Values Live On (hc), $23.95; (pb), $16.95   _____

_____ Spirit of Renewal (hc), $22.95; (pb), $16.95   _____

_____ A Time to Mourn (pb), $16.95   _____

_____ Tormented Master (pb), $17.95   _____

_____ Twelve Jewish Steps To Recovery, (hc) $19.95; (pb) $13.95   _____

_____ When a Grandparent Dies (hc), $14.95   _____

_____ Your Word Is Fire (pb), $14.95   _____

_____ Other:_____   _____

• The Kushner Series •

_____ The Book of Letters Popular Hardcover Edition (hc), $24.95   _____

_____ The Book of Words (hc), $21.95   _____

_____ God Was in This Place... (hc) $21.95; (pb) $16.95   _____

_____ Honey from the Rock (pb), $14.95   _____

_____ Invisible Lines of Connection (hc), $21.95   _____

_____ River of Light (pb), $14.95   _____

For s/h, add $3.50 for the first book, $2.00 each add'l book (to a max. of $12.00) $ s/h

TOTAL _____

Check enclosed for $ *payable to:* JEWISH LIGHTS Publishing

Charge my credit card: ❏ MasterCard   ❏ Visa   ❏ AMEX

Credit Card #_____ Expires _____

Name on card _____

Signature _____Phone (_____)_____

Name _____

Street _____

City / State / Zip _____

Phone, fax, or mail to: JEWISH LIGHTS Publishing

P. O. Box 237, Sunset Farm Offices, Route 4, Woodstock, Vermont 05091

Tel (802) 457-4000   *Fax* (802) 457-4004

Credit card orders (800) 962-4544 (9AM–5PM ET Monday–Friday)

Generous discounts on quantity orders. SATISFACTION GUARANTEED. Prices subject to change.

**AVAILABLE FROM BETTER BOOKSTORES.
TRY YOUR BOOKSTORE FIRST.**